René Descartes
DISCOURSE ON METHOD

Translated with an
Interpretive Essay by

Richard Kennington

Edited with Introduction,
Glossary, and Notes by

Pamela Kraus and **Frank Hunt**

Focus Publishing
Newburyport

Photo Credit : Portrait of Rene Descartes (1596-1650) (oil on canvas), French School, (17th century) / Musee des Augustins, Toulouse, France, / The Bridgeman Art Library International

ISBN 10: 1-58510-259-8
ISBN 978-1-58510-259-4

Printed in the United States of America
12 11 10 9 8 7 6 5 4 3

1014V

René Descartes
Discourse on Method

The Focus Philosophical Library

CONTENTS

EDITORS' NOTE

The *Discourse on the Method of Conducting One's Reason Well and Seeking Truth in the Sciences* was published anonymously at Leiden in June of 1637 together with the *Dioptrics*, the *Meteors*, and the *Geometry*, which are called on the title page "essays in this method." Of the title of the *Discourse*, Descartes wrote: "I do not put *Treatise on the Method* but *Discourse on the Method*, which is the same as *Preface* or *Notice Concerning the Method*, in order to show that I do not intend to teach the method, but solely to speak about it. For, as can be seen from what I say about it, it consists more in practice than in theory. And I name the following treatises *Essays in This Method* because I claim that the things they contain could not have been discovered without it, and because one can know by them what it is worth. So too I have inserted something of metaphysics, physics, and medicine in the preceding *Discourse*, in order to show that the method extends to all sorts of matters" (letter to Mersenne, 27 February 1637 [?]; AT 1:349).

Richard Kennington prepared more than one version of this translation before his death in 1999. We have edited and revised the translation in comparison with the original as printed in *Oeuvres de Descartes*, edited by Charles Adam and Paul Tannery, revised edition, 12 volumes (Paris: Vrin, 1964-76; abbreviated AT), 6:1-78. Pages of AT, volume 6, have been supplied in square brackets in the text. Where we have had to choose between consistency of translation and a slightly more idiomatic English, we have generally opted for the former. (For example, the expression *j'ose dire*, which might have been conveyed more idiomatically by "I venture to say," has been translated "I dare to say," in conformity with the translation of *oser* by "dare" elsewhere.) Our intention is to allow readers to follow important terms through the text. To take only one example, readers should be able to connect the discussion of "masters" in the beginning of Part 2 with the project of making ourselves "masters and possessors of nature" articulated in Part 6.

We have supplied a glossary, an index, and notes, some of which are indebted to Étienne Gilson, *Discours de la méthode, texte et commentaire*, sixth edition (Paris: Vrin, 1987). The interpretive essay was originally a lecture delivered in the Collegiate Lecture Series in the Liberal Arts at the University of Chicago on February 21, 1980. It was published in Richard Kennington, *On Modern Origins: Essays in Early Modern Philosophy*, edited by Pamela Kraus and Frank Hunt (Lanham: Lexington Books, 2004), 105-22, and is reprinted here by kind permission of the publisher.

The editors thank Janice Johnson, Terry and Annie Marshall, Sarah Navarre, Ron Pullins, Joe Sachs, John Tomarchio, Kathleen Blits, and an anonymous reader for Focus Publishing for their help with the translation and its publication.

Pamela Kraus and Frank Hunt
Annapolis and Santa Fe

INTRODUCTION

The *Discourse on Method* (1637) is a brief writing that serves as a "preface" to three scientific essays (the *Optics*, the *Geometry*, and the *Meteorology*).[1] Of the writings of René Descartes (1596-1650), it is the most widely read and is often assigned in university courses, both graduate and undergraduate, and across various disciplines—humanities, history, literature, rhetoric, history of science—as well as philosophy. Its popularity is in part a consequence of its author's renown. Descartes's singular contributions to philosophy, mathematics, and physics place him among the luminaries of his time. He simplified and augmented the power of mathematics through his discovery of analytic geometry; he formulated an account of nature as matter, and of matter as having qualities primarily geometrical in character, rendering it susceptible of mathematical treatment; he enumerated three laws of nature, by which all motions whatsoever are governed, inspiring a line of development to Isaac Newton; he redefined the soul, bequeathing us the notion of mind or consciousness, a domain marked off from that of body or matter; he made prominent a conception of philosophy in which this endeavor to understand the whole of things required prior reflection on and evaluation of the cognitive powers; and he thereby established the good of inquiry as accessible to many rather than restricted to the province of a few, and as beneficial for mankind rather than directed beyond human capability. The *Discourse on Method* succinctly describes all these contributions and their relation to one another.

Yet the *Discourse* is perhaps as much appreciated—and as noteworthy—for its form and style. It is by design not a treatise, but a "discourse" (Fr. *discours*), a word with a wider significance in the seventeenth century than today, meaning "talk" or "conversation."[2]

---

1   The *Discourse* itself runs to 78 pages in the critical edition of Descartes's works, AT 6.

2   Anne Sancier-Chateau, *Introduction à la langue du xviiᵉ siècle* (Paris: Èditions Nathan, 1993), 64.

1

Written in French, almost without technical terminology,[3] the *Discourse* addresses both philosophers or scientists and a popular audience, many of whom Descartes recognized would not either care to study or succeed in comprehending the accompanying scientific essays. As one commentator has put it, the *Discourse* is written "in two registers,"[4] and would seem to be a paradigm of the philosophy it espouses: nonacademic, productive, and available.

Yet the *Discourse* is not simply accessible. While its full title is *Discourse on the Method of Conducting One's Reason Well and Seeking Truth in the Sciences*, it lists without elaboration four rules of method and contains no sustained or developed arguments on any topic. Its longest continuous passage is that in Part 5 describing the circulation of the blood. Descartes tells his correspondent Marin Mersenne in 1637, "I do not put *Treatise on the Method* but *Discourse on the Method*, which is the same as *Preface* or *Notice Concerning the Method*, in order to show that I do not intend to teach the method, but solely to speak about it. For, as can be seen from what I say about it, it consists more in practice than in theory....I have inserted something of metaphysics, physics, and medicine...in order to show that the method extends to all sorts of matters."[5] Descartes, then, designs his preface as a summary so that the full power of his method should become evident, but withholds from the reader a full or direct presentation of it. Instead he conveys his thought in an autobiographical account. The narrator is not a pure mind standing behind a treatise on a recondite or rarified subject, or a philosopher speaking only to other philosophers, but a man speaking to all men, highlighting his endeavor to "acquire a clear and assured knowledge of all that is useful for life." As a man, of course, he is not just any man, as we quickly learn from Part 1 of the *Discourse*, but one whose great desire to learn and substantial particular gifts meet with good fortune and issue in significant if not revolutionary discoveries.

The *Discourse* is thus an interpretive challenge. Since it is not a treatise, it cannot be interpreted as if it were a treatise. Its discursive tone, its summary presentation, and its autobiographical character— all must be taken into account. For many it has proved to be difficult to do this, and thus to evaluate the *Discourse* and establish its place in Descartes's philosophy. Readers have found it challenging, for example,

---

3   A few Scholastic—that is, academic or scholarly—terms are italicized in the text.
4   Léon Brunschvicg, *Écrits philosophiques* (Paris: Presses Universitaires de France, 1951), 308. See, by contrast, William Harvey's introduction to his treatise on circulation, Galileo Galilei's to the *Dialogue Concerning the Two Chief World Systems*, and even Francis Bacon's to the *New Organon*.
5   AT 1:349.

to connect the methodical rules of Part 2 with the moral rules of Part 3 or to see the logic in separating the methodical themes in Part 2 from the metaphysical ones in Part 4, which seem to follow upon the adoption of methodical rules. There are still other anomalies in the text: for example, in Part 1, there is a criticism of Stoic virtue, but in Part 3, praise of and agreement with the Stoics; reason appears in Part 4 as a power to grasp certainties and in Part 5 as a "universal instrument." Some scholars account for these anomalies by arguing that the parts of the *Discourse*, or at least a version of them, were drafted at different times and only hastily put together in a preface. Indeed, many turn from the *Discourse* to the history of its composition and fill out or adjust the autobiography accordingly. Some even supplement this historical research by finding precedents in other authors for passages in the *Discourse*.[6] Frequently, however, these strategies substitute for an interpretation of the text, resulting in a reduction of the *Discourse* to a tissue of disparate strands held together only by the particular history of Descartes.

Yet even as a primarily historical record the *Discourse* is found wanting by some. It details the state of Descartes's thought up to 1633, but, or so it is claimed, in 1633 Descartes's philosophy was not in its definitive shape: however more comprehensive than other Cartesian writings the *Discourse* may be, it represents a stage on the way to his complete philosophy. This claim is usually based not on an interpretation of the *Discourse*, but on a preference given to later, more detailed, and more academic or traditionally "philosophical" presentations of Descartes's thought, such as we find in the *Meditations on First Philosophy* (1641). From this perspective, the *Discourse* appears of less consequence and therefore as less in need of interpretation. It is to open up the matter of the interpretation of the *Discourse* that we publish this translation with the appended essay.

We may begin to address the need by pointing to the fact that the *Discourse* itself directs us to consider the circumstances in which it was written and the import of contemporary events, for instance, the ongoing religious wars and the condemnation of Galileo Galilei. Thus the question of "context" is prominent from the beginning of the text, and, since the *Discourse* is Descartes's first publication, from the beginning of his public career, if we may use the word "public" of one

---

6 Descartes made rather free use of the works of others, adapting them to his own purposes, almost always without citation.

so jealous of his privacy.[7] He presents himself within his circumstances seeking both to surmount and to master them: he seeks the certain and the useful.

Descartes was born into an unsettled, even tumultuous and skeptical time. The rupture of Roman Catholic Christianity, underlined in the condemnation of Luther's writings in 1521, had spawned numerous Protestant sects and sometimes violent quarrels between Catholics and Protestants. Powerful political entities were aligned with different religious groups, Lutherans and Calvinists, for example, so as to vie with the temporal power of Rome. The Thirty Years' War (1618-48), to which Descartes alludes in Part 2 of the *Discourse*, was in fact a series of wars fought between the Habsburgs—the Catholic Holy Roman Emperors—and their various opponents, thus pitting rival Catholic and Protestant forces against one another, bringing civil war to the principalities of Germany, and spreading continual fighting throughout Europe.

It was also a time of intellectual ferment. Niccolò Machiavelli's *Prince*, presented to Lorenzo de Medici in 1513 and widely circulated before being published posthumously in 1532, purposely departed from any idealizing political philosophy of the past and openly avowed a political realism that drew on pagan, mainly Roman, rather than Christian examples. By 1557, *The Prince* was entered on the list of forbidden books by the Roman Catholic Church, a list referred to often simply as the "Index."[8] Michel de Montaigne in his *Essays*, which first appeared in three stages between 1580 and 1595, practiced his immense learning on himself and transformed the Socratic problem of ignorance and self-knowledge into an intimate yet universal skepticism. Nicolaus Copernicus's *On the Revolutions of the Celestial Orbits* (1543) upended Ptolemaic astronomy by placing the sun instead of the earth at the center of the cosmos: the earth was no longer stationary, but revolved along with other planets. The Ptolemaic structure, and the Aristotelian cosmology in agreement with it, had reigned for over a millennium and had become wedded to theological and religious beliefs; furthermore,

---

7   Descartes begins an early fragment: "Actors, taught not to let any embarrass-ment show on their faces, put on a mask. I will do the same. So far, I have been a spectator in this theater which is the world, but I am now about to mount the stage, and I come forward masked" (AT 10:213). Commenting on the censure of Galileo, Descartes quotes Ovid to Mersenne in a letter of April 1634: "I desire to live in peace and to continue the life I have begun under the motto 'Who has hidden well has lived well'" (AT 1:285-86).

8   Descartes says of *The Prince* in a letter to Princess Elisabeth of Bohemia, "I find in it many maxims which seem excellent....But there are also many others which I can-not approve" (AT 4:486). Of Machiavelli's *Discourses on Livy*, he says that he "found nothing bad in it" (AT 4:531).

it was the framework that most accorded with ordinary perception. The Copernican theory overturned this framework and so destroyed for many their fundamental sense of place and proportion with respect to nature and to God. The invention of the telescope, probably in early 1600 in Holland, made it possible to provide heretofore unavailable evidence for heliocentrism; and Galileo announced just such evidence in *The Starry Messenger* (1610): he had observed moons revolving around Jupiter.

The revolution in the understanding of the heavens begun by Galileo and advanced by Johannes Kepler brought with it new understandings of terrestrial matters, that is to say, of bodies and their motions. In his classic *New Organon* (1620), Francis Bacon repudiated the order of inquiry established in the wake of Aristotle's natural science and logic, and proposed instead of a merely "theoretical" physics with no apparent concern to explain particular phenomena an experimental method geared to the controlled observation, recognition, and organizing of qualities common to many kinds of bodies and to the explanation of their behavior in terms of the motions of minimal parts. William Gilbert studied the extraordinary, and to some (including Gilbert himself) spiritual, properties of the magnet; and, in 1628, William Harvey published his account of the heart and its role in the circulation of the blood, replacing the Galenic theory that had dominated the course of study in medical schools.

Thus in the early seventeenth century, European political, religious, social, and scientific traditions were in the midst of a major transition and disruption that threatened to terminate their dominance. Philosophers took account of and participated in the new directions of thought— philosophy and science were not regarded as distinct at this time—and began to part with or reinterpret those elements of the philosophical tradition with which these directions were incompatible, primarily the theologico-philosophical development of Aristotelian metaphysics and physics that governed the universities or "Schools." That new departures were needed and being embarked upon; that new avenues of inquiry were being avidly pursued; that new possibilities of explanation and achievement were imagined; that the most fundamental issues, that is to say, those about nature and ourselves and God, were being rethought— all of this made the time both exciting and unquiet, and beckoning to Descartes, whose ability was of the first rank and whose desire for knowledge was "extreme."[9]

The *Discourse on Method* is Descartes's first publication but

---

9   See *Discourse*, Part 1 (AT 6:4.24).

it is neither the first thing he wrote nor the first for publication. In 1637 Descartes was forty-one years old—he died shortly before his fifty-fourth birthday—but he had been thinking and writing about science and philosophy since his early twenties and had attempted a comprehensive treatment of his thought in 1628. In the unfinished "little book,"[10] *Rules for the Direction of the Native Intelligence*, "method" is in a prominent place. Others had, of course, prescribed a method or general rules of thought before Descartes, and some, like Bacon, had combined it with a critique of traditional ways of inquiry, but Descartes's *Rules* presented a critique of traditional learning that pointed to the need for method, proposed rules of method, and wedded the methodical reasoning to distinctively mathematical inquiries, which no one before him had done. In the *Rules*, he reflects on and reasons about the use of method in all domains of inquiry, so that some have even credited him with a decisive contribution to the mathematization of nature.[11]

Teachings in the *Rules* have some obvious correlations in the *Discourse*. The *Rules* begins with a statement of purpose, in which we see that from the earliest Descartes aimed at a comprehensive unification of the sciences that would allow both the pleasure of contemplation and practical benefit. The possibility of that unification was grounded in certitude, specifically in the natural ability of the mind to grasp truths that are present to it apart from the senses (the term in the *Rules* is "intuition"). This sort of certitude provided a basis for method, or methodical reasoning, as opposed to reasoning based on erroneous sources—"the fluctuating testimony of the senses or the deceptive judgment of the imagination."[12] As early as the *Rules* Descartes saw that evident truths included not only arithmetical and geometrical propositions, but others relating to self-knowledge: he observes in Rule 3 that "everyone can mentally intuit that he exists, that he thinks," but does not single out these propositions or endow them with more

---

10 See Rule 4, where he refers to *hoc libello* (AT 10:379).

11 Edmund Husserl, *The Crisis of European Sciences* (trans. David Carr [Evanston: Northwestern University Press, 1970]), analyzes the transformation of nature we have called "mathematization" focusing primarily on Galileo, with whom, he says, "the idea in question appears for the first time, so to speak, as full-blown; thus I have linked all our considerations to his name, in a certain sense simplifying and idealizing the matter" (57). Galileo did not explicitly provide the conceptual framework or the theory of matter that underlies the transformation. See on this point Jacob Klein, *Greek Mathematical Thought and the Origin of Algebra*, trans. Eva Brann (Cambridge: MIT Press, 1968), and the essay on Klein by Burt Hopkins, "Meaning and Truth in Klein's Philosophico-Mathematical Writings," *The St. John's Review* 48/3 (2005): 57-88.

12 See Rule 3 (AT 10:368).

significance until they reappear in Part 4 of the *Discourse*.

The term "method" points to a problem and to a solution. The problem, as it is presented in the *Rules*, is that the mind's natural ability to witness certitude is not supported by a natural ability to direct itself in the pursuit of knowledge. Put another way, the difficulty is that our most ordinary access to the world, through sensation, is not reliable; consequently, any way of reasoning, any organon, or any pursuit of knowledge that depends on or derives from sensation is misleading. The solution is the discovery—or devising—of an art, new and reliable rules of procedure to replace long-established practices such as those based on Aristotle's logical works.[13] In the *Discourse*, this diagnosis and prescription is conducted in Parts 1 and 2, but in an autobiographical mode. Among all the disciplines, certitude is found in mathematical knowledge, and the rules of method that emerge from a reflection on perfection summarize those enunciated in Rules 5 through 7. In the *Rules*, these methodical rules of procedure are said to need elaboration, so that they will be able to apply to all sorts of inquiry. They do not suffice by themselves, but must be developed and brought to bear on mathematical problems; mathematical operations, in turn, are understood essentially as the relation of magnitudes of whatever kind to one another. Subsequently, these procedures are to be applied to problems involving natural bodies. The essay *Geometry*, which follows the *Discourse*, lays out the finished mathematical product, while a physics susceptible of mathematical treatment is described in *The World*, written between 1629 and 1633, and summarized in *Discourse* Part 5.

The comprehensiveness of Descartes's earliest ambition and the revolutionary character of method are nowhere more evident than in the attention he gives to the whole of human knowledge. Before he even fills out the rules or applies them to particular scientific problems, he first attempts to complete the fundamental "turn" his methodical philosophy embodies. Since the native power of mind is reliable but the powers of sensation and imagining are not, and have led to mere "wanderings" rather than truth, some methodical account is needed of how and to what extent knowledge—knowledge of nature in particular—is possible. Descartes struggles with how best to formulate the project to inquire into the "nature and scope of knowledge" in Rule 8, which appears to be a composite of three drafts. In Rule 12, he sketches a doctrine of the mind and its powers that anticipates the mechanical account we find elaborated in the *Treatise on Man* (1629-

---

13   See Rule 2 (AT 10:363) and Rule 10 (AT 10:405-6), where Descartes criticizes the logic of the Schools.

33). [14] While it is an anachronism to call what Descartes offers here and in later writings "epistemology," it is clear that the need to delineate the extent of the mind's powers as a distinctive discipline has roots in the contention that we need methodical inquiry.

Descartes abandoned the *Rules* some time around 1628, possibly to remedy its defects and fill in the lacunae of his knowledge. Among them we mention only the most obvious: the goal of inquiry, while universal in intention, is not made fully clear; a mechanistic account of perception is merely imported into the account and little attention is paid to its relation to the intuitive power of mind; there is no doctrine of matter, much less one that would support the extension of methodical procedures to the understanding of bodies; and, although he belittles the Aristotelian definition of motion, Descartes provides no definition or description of motion to replace it.

Between 1629 and 1633 Descartes worked assiduously on various aspects of his thought, including those aspects missing from the *Rules*. He wrote a treatise on meteorology; worked on a theory of optics; formulated a mechanistic description of the functions of the human body, adding to the now-expanded physiological psychology of perception briefly described in the *Rules* vital and motive functions, such as respiration, nutrition, circulation, and reaction to stimuli; and began to draft "a little treatise of Metaphysics." [15] The essentials of this treatise, "to prove the existence of God and of our souls, when they are separated from our bodies, from which follows their immortality," appear in Part 4 of the *Discourse on Method*. Other letters during that time indicate that he had in mind to explain "the whole of physics" [16] and began to design his account. In April 1630 he wrote to Mersenne that he had laid aside treatises he began in Paris because "while I was working on them I acquired a little more knowledge than I had when beginning them, and when I tried to accommodate them, I was constrained to start a new project a little larger than the first." [17] The abandoned work may refer in part to the *Rules* or portions of it; the "new project" most likely was the beginning of the treatise that we know as *The World*, which he prepared for publication aiming at 1633.

---

14 He includes in Rule 12 a chart that seems to have been borrowed from a description in Bacon's *Valerius Terminus*. See AT 10:413 and Francis Bacon, *Valerius Terminus*, chap. 11, in *The Works of Francis Bacon*, ed. James Spedding, Robert Leslie Ellis, and Douglas Denon Heath, vol. 3 (London: Longmans, 1870), 237. The *Treatise on Man* was originally intended to be part of the larger work *The World*, which Descartes drafted but chose to summarize in Part 5 of the *Discourse* rather than publish.

15 See the letter to Mersenne, 25 November 1630 (AT 1:82).

16 To Mersenne, 13 November 1629 (AT 1:70).

17 To Mersenne, 15 April 1630 (AT 1:137-38).

The World was planned to be a mechanistic science of nature, a cosmology in which the heavenly bodies—the fixed stars as well as planets, comets, and other celestial phenomena—and all bodies on earth, including phenomena such as tides, would be explained using the same principles and laws. Descartes had defined nature as "matter," and matter he defined as extension in length, breadth, and depth, a "geometrical" understanding that owed nothing to ordinary sensation. Matter thus understood is quantifiable and contains nothing that "anyone"[18] cannot understand. Matter has parts but not atomic parts; rather, it is divisible into three general classes, which he calls "elements," distinguished in terms of size, speed, and shape. The motions of matter are all to be explained in terms of local motion alone; and local motion is understood inertially, that is to say, once present in a body, motion is altered only by collision, and when unimpeded, bodies tend to motion in straight lines. Natural motion, then, is not teleological motion, as the Aristotelian and some of the Scholastic tradition had assumed; rather, it is governed by three "laws of nature," established by God. Obedient to these laws, the world of heavens, earth, and all intervening material came to be, with centers around which the material moved, so that the earth revolves around the sun. The comprehensive science of motion was also to explain as local motions or the effects of local motions all functions and activities of animal life, especially human functions once attributed to the soul, such as sensation, imagination, hunger, thirst, and dreams.[19] Descartes's account spells out each of these functions, incorporating diagrams of human anatomy. There is evidence that *The World* is missing two chapters that would have connected the cosmology, which in the manuscript ends at Chapter 15, with the portion beginning to treat of human beings, which begins at Chapter 18. Thus the section that provided the all-important link between the mechanistic cosmology and the mechanistic anthropology is missing.[20]

---

18 "Now, since we are taking the liberty of imagining this matter to our fancy, let us attribute to it, if you will, a nature in which there is absolutely nothing that anyone cannot know as perfectly as possible." *Le monde*, trans. Michael Sean Mahoney (New York: Abaris Books, 1979), 51-53 (AT 11:33.4-8).

19 Aristotle, *De Anima* 2.2, 413b10: "the soul is the source of these things that have been mentioned and is defined by them: by nutrition, by sense perception, by thinking things through, and by motion." *Aristotle's On the Soul and On Memory and Recollection*, trans. Joe Sachs (Santa Fe: Green Lion Press, 2001).

20 T. S. Hall in the introduction to his edition of the *Treatise of Man* says: "There is unassailable evidence that a passage of uncertain length and contents, connecting the two, is missing. A third part, which would probably have borne the title *Of the Soul*, was planned and probably drafted. It may have been destroyed by Descartes himself." *Treatise of Man*, ed. T. S. Hall (Cambridge: Harvard University Press, 1972), xxiv. See also Adam's introduction in AT 11:3-4. No draft has ever been found.

In 1632 Galileo published the *Dialogue Concerning the Two Chief World Systems*, a defense of Copernicanism, which the Pope had forbidden him to pursue in 1616. In 1633 Galileo's book was put on the Index, and he was required to abjure his "heresy" by the Holy Office of the Roman Catholic Church. As a result of the condemnation of Galileo, Descartes decided in November 1633 to withhold his treatise from publication. *The World* did not appear until after Descartes's death, in two parts, one called *The World, or Treatise on Light*, and the other *Treatise on Man*.[21]

The World together with the *Treatise on Man*—that is to say, the treatise minus the missing chapters—espouses a universal mechanistic materialism. Unlike ancient materialism—for example, the Lucretian account we find in *On the Nature of Things*—*The World* propounds no atoms and no void, and it contains no "swerve." It weds a corpuscular mechanism to a law-governed mathematical physics and proposes a divine source for matter, for the beginning of motion, and for the establishment of the laws of motion.

The treatise was, then, a challenge to orthodox philosophy. In *The World* Descartes explicitly identifies "philosophers" with Aristotelian and Scholastico-Aristotelian themes: the doctrine of the four elements; the notion of prime matter (a matter divested of all qualities); the definition of motion as "the actuality of the potential insofar as it is potential," taken over from Book 3 of Aristotle's *Physics*; the medieval doctrine of an infinite void beyond the cosmos; and the recognition of other sorts of motion besides local motion (alteration, growth and decline, and coming to be and passing away), all of which Descartes reduces to mechanical motion. Perhaps even more seriously given the religious climate, Descartes's account of the world opposes or at least requires that one reinterpret the Biblical account of creation: the God of *The World* is not easily identified with the God of the Bible. To counter this problem, beginning with Chapter 6, Descartes wrote the account of the world—the "new world" which comes to be ordered as a result of God's having established laws and having set in motion the matter he has created—as a "fable," a word he uses about his own autobiography in the *Discourse*.

Descartes did not immediately give up the idea of publishing the treatise. In one letter in 1634 he says he hopes that his treatise will see

---

21   The *Treatise on Man* was first published in Latin at Leiden in 1662; Descartes's friend Claude Clerselier produced French versions of the two parts, *Le monde* and *L'homme*, which were published separately in 1664. The two have recently been published in one volume with critical notes and commentary: René Descartes, *Le monde; L'homme*, ed. Annie Bitbol-Hespériès and Jean-Pierre Verdet (Paris: Éditions du Seuil, 1996).

the light of day; in 1635 he sent the treatise to Constantijn Huygens, but he wrote to him later that he planned to publish the *Meteorology* with the *Optics*, and add a preface to them.²² He then added to these essays the *Geometry* and prefaced them with the *Discourse on Method*.

The *Discourse on Method* is in fact a summary of virtually every avenue of thought that Descartes had pursued and written about previously and some he had not. Part 1 surveys the educational situation in Europe, criticizing the state of learning in which only mathematics is certain and no learning is useful. In light of this, Part 2 begins with a reflection on the standard of perfection, which leads, in turn, to the devising of method and to the listing of four rules summarized from the *Rules*. It also describes briefly Descartes's mathematical discoveries, the most outstanding of which, as has been noted, are exemplified in the appended *Geometry*. Part 3 adds a dimension to Descartes's thought, in that it describes four moral "rules" or "maxims," which include one prescribing the best choice of life, that of "cultivating reason." In Part 4, drawing perhaps on the little treatise on metaphysics he claimed to be drafting in 1630, Descartes sustains doubt of the senses and eventually elevates the intuited certainty mentioned in the *Rules* into the "first principle of [his] philosophy," "I think, therefore I am." He argues on the basis of this principle that the soul is completely distinct from the body, and he contends that one can reason to the existence of God, who ultimately guarantees the certainty of what we accept as true. In Part 5, he summarizes *The World*, the cosmology as well as the wholly mechanical account of the circulation of the blood, along with a brief synopsis of the mechanics of perception. Descartes alludes to the reasons for his suppression of *The World* (he returns to the subject in the opening lines of Part 6), and identifies the distinguishing difference of humans from other animals—the versatility of reason as a universal instrument. He returns to the subject of the soul, claiming that it is not derivable from the power of matter. Finally, in Part 6, he characterizes his philosophy: it is not the traditional theoretical philosophy but a practical one that promises great benefits to mankind, such as the enjoyment of the "fruits of the earth," and "health," which is "the primary good," benefits that he formulates as rendering us like "masters and possessors of nature"; and he details the course of his decision to publish.

Publication of the *Discourse* provoked reaction, but no part provoked more than Part 4. Descartes returned to the "meditations" described in the *Discourse* as "so metaphysical and so uncommon" and published an extensive treatment of them in the *Meditations on First*

---

22 To Mersenne, April 1634 (AT 1:288); 1 November 1635 (AT 1:591-92).

Philosophy. The *Meditations* is a treatise[23] that challenged the power of reason as it had not been previously challenged, claiming that an omnipotent God could deceive us even in what appears indubitable. It thus emphasized the dependence of scientific knowledge on God and God's goodness, so that a theological metaphysics now appeared to supervene on and even negate rational certitude as the foundation for knowledge. The subsequent *Principles of Philosophy* (1644) returned to the themes of the *Meditations* in its first part, while the three remaining parts provided an exposition of the Cartesian physics from *The World*, with some additions, including laws of collision. In the Preface to the French edition of the *Principles*, Descartes describes his philosophy thus: "The whole of philosophy is like a tree of which the roots are metaphysics, the trunk is physics, and the branches that rise from this trunk are all the other sciences, which can be reduced to three principal ones, namely, medicine, mechanics, and morals."[24] This tree is an image of the "systematic" character of Descartes's philosophy: metaphysics is prior to and the source of all and yet method appears nowhere. In that Preface he describes the *Discourse*, but in an attenuated fashion. Now, instead of a showcase for the power of reason and the benefits of method, he describes it as the place where he "summarized the principal rules of logic and an imperfect morality, which one could follow provisionally."[25]

The *Meditations* and the *Principles* are not without their own interpretive difficulties, however, difficulties that call into question the simple superiority of these treatises over the more comprehensive presentation of the *Discourse*.[26] The exploration of the relation between these metaphysical texts and the *Discourse* goes to the heart of the Cartesian enterprise and, of course, to our understanding of it. Does that enterprise require the support of a divine guarantee of truth and do its subsequent parts stem from a metaphysics of substance, which would place Descartes's thought within the tradition of a theoretical, metaphysical philosophy? Or is Descartes's philosophy designed and established from the outset to arrive at effective knowledge, so that its parts and their relation must be seen first and foremost in light of this purpose? In this case, philosophy is more a human construction

---

23   AT 7:4, *in hoc Tractatu*.

24   AT 9/2:14.

25   AT 9/2:15. After the *Discourse* the term "method" virtually drops out of Descartes's published writings. An interesting occurrence is a passage in the Letter to the Sorbonne that precedes the *Meditations*, claiming that in this work he will "make trial" of the method.

26   See Richard Kennington, "The 'Teaching of Nature' in Descartes's Soul Doctrine," in *On Modern Origins*, ed. Pamela Kraus and Frank Hunt (Lanham: Lexington Books, 2004), 161-86.

using natural resources to overcome the deficiencies of nature. Or is his philosophy some amalgam of the two?

These issues cannot be explored unless the *Discourse* is first seen as a whole. The essay that follows this translation is an introductory description of this wholeness. The author accepts as one interpretive principle Descartes's assertion in Part 1 that "I offer this writing only as a history, or if you prefer, as a fable," and supplements it with the interpretive advice Descartes himself rather swiftly provides when he speaks of the advantages and disadvantages of these genres.[27] The interpretive essay advises that we read the *Discourse* with the appropriate caution: with an eye to the narrative presentation of a summary aimed at two audiences, the general public and the scientific or learned community. Descartes's narrative turns out to be not a personal memoir or a mere history, but a structured account of an unrepeatable and exemplary life that presents the parts of Cartesian philosophy and their relation to one another.

The *Discourse on Method* welcomes the public into a new view of the scientific or philosophical life and of its power to benefit all, if only it can be conducted freely. This freedom to inquire and to carry out necessary experiments requires a mind uncompromised by false opinions, aided by good health and a good purpose, and, what is more, supported by tolerant regimes and the general public.[28]

In his last writing, *The Passions of the Soul* (1649), Descartes again returns to the subject of the soul, emphasizing those functions that are dependent on the body, most especially the passions, whose "principal effect" is to "incite and dispose their soul to will the things for which they prepare their body," primarily actions to protect and preserve ourselves.[29] That writing contains an overview of the powers of the soul, but nowhere in it is there an argument for the metaphysical independence of mind, and the intellective power of the soul, which that argument presupposes, receives perhaps only a passing allusion. *The Passions of the Soul* can be linked more directly to themes in the *Discourse on Method* and to the discussion of the human composite in Part 6 of the *Meditations*, of which it is an elaboration.

Pamela Kraus

---

27 "The gracefulness of fables awakens the mind" but "fables make us imagine many things as possible that are not"; and "histories…if read with discretion…help to form judgment" yet "even the most faithful histories…almost always omit the most base and least illustrious circumstances" (AT 6:5-7).

28 See Richard Kennington, "Descartes and Mastery of Nature" and "René Descartes," in *On Modern Origins*, 123-44, 187-204.

29 AT 11:359.

DISCOURSE ON THE METHOD OF CONDUCTING ONE'S REASON WELL AND SEEKING TRUTH IN THE SCIENCES

If this discourse seems too long to be read at one time, it can be divided into six parts. In the first will be found various considerations concerning the sciences. In the second, the principal rules of the method the author has sought. In the third, some of the rules of the morality that he has drawn from this method. In the fourth, the reasons by which he proves the existence of God and of the human soul, which are the foundations of his metaphysics. In the fifth, the order of questions of physics that he has sought, and particularly the explanation of the movement of the heart and some other difficulties that belong to medicine, as well as the difference between our soul and that of the beasts. And in the last, some things he believes required for advancing further in the study of nature than he has gone, and the reasons that have made him write.

PART 1

Good sense is the best distributed thing in the world, for everyone thinks he is so well provided with it that [2] even those who are most difficult to content in all other things do not customarily desire more than they have.[1] In this it is improbable that all are deceived; rather,

---

1   The thought expressed in this sentence is already cited as proverbial by Michel de Montaigne (1533-92) in *Essays* 2.17, "Of Presumption": "It is commonly said that the fairest division of her favors Nature has given us is that of sense; for there is no one who is not content with the share of it that she has allotted him" (*The Complete Essays of Montaigne*, trans. Donald M. Frame [Stanford: Stanford University Press, 1958], 499). Étienne Gilson's *Discours de la méthode, texte et commentaire*, 6th ed. (Paris: Vrin, 1987), identifies other passages or terms in the *Discourse* that recall or adapt Montaigne (for example, "the great book of the world").

this testifies that the power of judging well and of distinguishing the true from the false, which is properly what is called good sense or reason, is naturally equal in all men, and thus that the diversity of our opinions arises not because some are more reasonable than others, but only because we conduct our thoughts by different ways, and do not consider the same things. For it is not enough to have a good mind,[2] but the principal thing is to apply it well. The greatest souls are capable of the greatest vices as well as the greatest virtues, and those who only walk very slowly can advance much further, if they always follow the right path, than those who run and go astray.

As for myself, I have never presumed that the perfection of my mind was in any way uncommon; indeed I have often wished my thought was as quick, my imagination as clear [nette] and distinct, or my memory as wide and prompt as that of some others. And I know of no other qualities than these that make for the perfection of mind. For as to reason, or sense, inasmuch as it alone makes us men, and distinguishes us from the beasts, I would like to believe that it is complete in each of us, and in this regard to follow the common opinion of the philosophers, who say that there is more or less only among [3] accidents, and not among the forms, or natures, of the individuals of the same species.[3]

But I do not fear to say that I think I have had the good fortune during my youth to have fallen into certain paths that led me to considerations and maxims from which I formed a method[4] by which, it seems to me, I have a means of augmenting my knowledge by degrees, and of elevating it little by little to the highest point to which the mediocrity of my mind and the short duration of my life will permit. For I have already gathered such fruits from it that, although in the judgments I make of myself I always try to lean toward the side of mistrust rather than that of presumption, and although when looked at with the eye of a philosopher almost none of the diverse actions and enterprises of men do not seem to me vain and useless, I do not fail to receive an extreme satisfaction from the progress I think I have already made in the search for truth, and to conceive such hopes for the future that if, among the occupations of men purely as men, there is any that is solidly good and important, I dare to believe that it is the one that I have chosen.

Nevertheless, it may be that I deceive myself, and it is perhaps only a little copper and glass that I am taking for gold and diamonds. I know

---

2   See Glossary, s.v. "Mind."
3   The words in italics are common metaphysical terms found in Scholastic philosophy and theology, the medieval tradition of learning dominant in the universities and colleges. See Glossary, s.v. "Schools."
4   See Glossary, s.v. "Method."

how subject we are to error in what concerns ourselves, and also how much we must suspect the judgments of our friends when they are in our favor. But I will be glad to show in this discourse [4] what paths I have followed, and to represent my life in it as in a picture, so that each may judge of it, and I will have, by learning the opinions about it from the common report, a new means of instruction to add to those I customarily use.

Thus it is not my intention here to teach the method that each should follow to conduct his reason well, but only to show in what fashion I have tried to conduct my own. Those who take it upon themselves to give precepts must regard themselves as more capable than those to whom they give them, and if they fail in the least thing, they are blamable. But since I offer this writing only as a history, or if you prefer, as a fable, in which, among some examples that can be imitated, there will perhaps be found also many others that it will not be right to follow, I hope that it will be useful to some without being harmful to anyone, and that everyone will be grateful for my frankness.

I was nourished on letters from childhood, and because I was persuaded that by their means one could acquire a clear and assured knowledge of all that is useful for life, I had an extreme desire to learn them. But as soon as I had finished that whole course of studies at the end of which one is customarily received into the ranks of the learned, I changed my opinion entirely. For I found myself embarrassed with so many doubts[5] and errors that there seemed to me to have been no other benefit in trying to instruct myself except that I had discovered more and more my own ignorance. And yet [5] I was in one of the most celebrated schools of Europe,[6] where I thought there must be some learned men if there were any in any place on earth. I had learned there all that others learned there, and not being content with those sciences[7] that they taught us, I had even looked through all the books that fell into my hands treating of the sciences considered most curious and most rare.[8] Moreover, I knew the judgments others made of me, and I did not see that I was esteemed inferior to my fellow students, although there were already some among them destined to fill the places of our masters.[9] And finally our age seemed to me as flourishing and as fertile in good minds as any of the preceding. Therefore I took the liberty of

5   See Glossary, s.v. "Doubt."
6   Descartes attended the Jesuit college of La Flèche at Anjou for about nine years, beginning around 1606 or 1607.
7   See Glossary, s.v. "Science."
8   Descartes refers to alchemy, astrology, and other occult sciences.
9   See Glossary, s.v. "Master."

judging all others by myself, and of thinking that there was no doctrine in the world such as I had previously been led to hope for.

I did not, however, cease to respect the exercises that occupy one in the schools. I knew that the languages we learn there are necessary for the understanding of ancient books; that the gracefulness of fables awakens the mind; that the memorable actions of histories elevate it, and that if they are read with discretion, they help to form judgment; that the reading of all good books is like a conversation with the finest men of past ages, who are their authors, and even a studied conversation, in which they unfold to us only the best of their thoughts; that eloquence has incomparable powers and beauties; that poetry has [6] most enchanting refinements and sweetness; that mathematics has very subtle discoveries that are of great service, whether for contenting the curious or for facilitating all the arts and reducing human toil; that the writings that treat of morals contain many teachings and exhortations to virtue that are very useful; that theology teaches us how to get to heaven; that philosophy supplies a means of talking plausibly about everything, and of making oneself admired by the less learned; that jurisprudence, medicine, and the other sciences afford honors and riches to those who cultivate them; and, finally, that it is good to have examined them all, even the most superstitious and false, in order to know their just worth and to keep from being deceived by them.

But I believed I had already given enough time to languages, and even to the reading of ancient books, to their histories as well as their fables. For conversing with those of other ages is almost the same as traveling. It is good to know something of the morals of different peoples in order to judge more sanely of our own and not think that what is contrary to our modes is ridiculous and against reason, as those who have seen nothing usually do. But one who employs too much time traveling finally becomes a stranger in his own country, and one who becomes too curious about things practiced in past ages ordinarily remains very ignorant of those practiced in this one. Besides which, fables make us imagine many things [7] as possible that are not, and even the most faithful histories, if they do not change or augment the value of things in order to render them more worthy of being read, at least almost always omit the most base and least illustrious circumstances, so that what remains does not appear such as it is, and those who regulate their morals by the examples they draw from them are likely to fall into the extravagances of the knights-errant of our romances,[10] and to conceive purposes that surpass their powers.

---

10   Knights-errant (*paladins*): originally, legendary heroes of the court of Charlemagne or King Arthur; by extension, any hero of a romance (Gilson, *Discours*, 123).

I held eloquence in high esteem, and I was enamored of poetry, but I thought that both were gifts of mind rather than fruits of study. Those who have the strongest reasoning capacity, and who best digest their thoughts in order to make them clear and intelligible, are always the best able to persuade others of what they propose, although they speak only low Breton and have never learned rhetoric. And those who have the most agreeable conceits, and who know how to express them with the most adornment and sweetness, would not fail to be the best poets even though they were ignorant of the poetic art.

I was above all pleased with the mathematical sciences because of the certitude and evidence[11] of their arguments, but I did not yet perceive their true use, and thinking they were only of service to the mechanical arts, I was astonished that since their foundations were so firm and solid nothing more exalted had been built on them. On the other hand, I compared the moral writings of the ancient pagans to splendid and magnificent palaces [8] built only on sand and mud. They exalt the virtues to the heights, and make them appear more estimable than everything in the world, but they do not sufficiently teach how to know them, and often what they call by such a beautiful name is only insensibility, or pride, or despair, or parricide.[12]

I revered our theology, and aspired as much as anyone to reach heaven, but having learned as an assured thing that the way to heaven is open to the most ignorant no less than to the most learned, and that the revealed truths that lead us there are above our intelligence, I would not have dared to submit them to the feebleness of my reasonings, and I thought that in order to undertake to examine them and to succeed, I would need to have some extraordinary assistance from heaven, and to be more than a man.

I will say nothing of philosophy except that, seeing that it has been cultivated by the most excellent minds who have lived in many ages, and that nevertheless nothing is found in it that is not in dispute and consequently that is not doubtful, I did not have enough presumption to hope for better success there than others. And considering that there can be diverse opinions about the same matter maintained by learned people without it being possible for more than one to be true, I regarded almost as false that which was only probable.

Then, as for the other sciences, inasmuch as they draw their principles from philosophy, I judged [9] that nothing solid could have

---

11 See Glossary, s.v. "Evidence."
12 Descartes alludes to Stoic doctrines of virtue and happiness. Stoicism had under-
    gone a resurgence of interest in the sixteenth century. Descartes addresses the
    thought of the Stoics again in Part 3 below.

been built on such unfirm foundations. And neither the honor nor the gain that they promise was sufficient to incite me to learn them, for I felt that my situation, thanks be to God, did not oblige me to make a trade of science in order to alleviate my fortune, and although I did not make a profession of disdaining glory like the cynics, nevertheless I cared little for what I could hope to gain only by false titles. And finally, as regards evil doctrines, I thought I already knew sufficiently what they were worth, so as not to be deceived by the promises of an alchemist, the predictions of an astrologer, the impostures of a magician, or the artifices and the boasting of those who make a profession of knowing more than they do.

That is why, as soon as age permitted me to escape the subjection of my preceptors, I gave up the study of letters completely. Resolving to seek no other science but that which could be found in myself, or else in the great book of the world, I used the rest of my youth to travel, to see courts and armies, to frequent people of diverse humors and conditions, to collect various experiences,[13] to test myself in the encounters that fortune offered me, and everywhere to make such reflection on the things that presented themselves as would profit me. For it seemed to me that I could encounter much more truth in the reasonings that each makes about the affairs that concern him, and whose outcome [10] must punish him immediately afterwards if he has judged badly, than in those made by a man of letters in his study in speculations that produce no effect, and that have no other consequence for him except perhaps that he will derive more vanity from them the more they are removed from common sense, because he will have had to employ so much more mind and artifice in attempting to render them probable. And I always had an extreme desire to learn to distinguish the true from the false in order to see clearly in my actions, and to walk with assurance in this life.

It is true that, while I did nothing but observe the morals of other men, I found scarcely anything there to convince me, and I noticed almost as much diversity in them as I had previously found in the opinions of the philosophers. So that the greatest profit I derived from this was that, seeing many things that, although they seem most extravagant and ridiculous to us, do not fail to be commonly received and approved by other great peoples, I learned not to believe too firmly anything of which I had been persuaded only by example and custom, and thus I liberated myself little by little from many errors that may obscure our natural light and render us less capable of listening to reason. But after I had spent several years in thus studying the book of the world and

---

13   See Glossary, s.v. "Experience."

in trying to acquire some experience, I resolved one day also to study within myself, and to use all the forces of my mind to choose the paths that I should follow. I succeeded much [11] better in this, it seems to me, than if I had never left either my country or my books.

PART 2

I was then in Germany, where the occasion of the wars that are not yet ended had called me. And as I was returning to the army from the coronation of the emperor,[14] the onset of winter halted me in a region where, not finding any conversation that diverted me, and also, by good fortune, not having any cares or passions[15] that disturbed me, I remained all day long shut up alone in a heated room, where I had complete leisure to converse with my thoughts. Among these, one of the first that I was drawn to consider was that often there is less perfection in works composed of several pieces and made by the hand of diverse masters than in those at which one alone has worked. Thus one sees that buildings undertaken and completed by a single architect are customarily more beautiful and better ordered than those that several have tried to refashion by making use of old walls that had been built for other ends. Thus those ancient towns that were mere villages in the beginning and became great cities in the course of time are usually so badly arranged in comparison with those regular cities that an engineer lays out as he wishes on a plain that, although when we consider their edifices individually, we often find in them as much or more art than in those of others, nevertheless when we see how they are arranged— here a great building, there a little one—and how they render the streets curved and uneven, we [12] would say that it is fortune rather than the will of men using reason that has so disposed them. And if we consider that nonetheless there have been at all times some officials responsible for making the buildings of individuals serve as an ornament to the public, we will recognize that it is difficult, if we only labor upon the works of others, to do things that are well executed. Thus I imagined that the peoples who, having formerly been half-savage and having become civilized only little by little, made their laws only insofar as

---

14 The wars are those occurring at the outset of what came to be known as the Thirty Years' War (1618-48). These were a series of primarily religious wars between Catholics and Protestants begun in Germany but ultimately involving most countries of Europe. Descartes refers to the coronation of the Holy Roman Emperor Ferdinand II in 1619 at Frankfurt. Ferdinand was a Catholic and leader of the Counter-Reformation.
15 See Glossary, s.v. "Passion."

the inconvenience of crimes and quarrels forced them to do so cannot be so well governed as those who have observed the enactments of some prudent legislator since they were first assembled. Similarly, it is quite certain that the state of the true religion, whose ordinances have been made by God alone, must be incomparably better regulated than all others. And to speak of human things, I believe that if Sparta was formerly very flourishing, this was not because of the goodness of each of its laws in particular, since many were quite strange and even contrary to good morals, but because they all tended to the same end, having been discovered by one alone.[16] And thus I thought that the sciences of books, at least those whose reasons are only probable, and that contain no demonstrations, having been composed and enlarged little by little by the opinions of diverse persons, do not come so close to the truth as the simple reasonings that a man of good sense can make naturally [13] about the things that present themselves. And hence I also thought that, because we have all been children before being men, and because it was necessary for us to be governed for a long time by our appetites and our preceptors, which were often contrary to one another, and neither of which perhaps counseled us always for the best, it is almost impossible for our judgments to be so pure and solid as they would have been if we had had the entire use of our reason from our birth and had always been conducted only by it.

It is true that we do not see one tearing down all the houses of a city for the sole purpose of remaking them in a different manner and of making the streets more beautiful. But one does see that many tear down their own houses in order to rebuild them, and that sometimes they are even compelled to do so, when they are in danger of falling of themselves, or when the foundations are not very firm. This example persuaded me that it was truly implausible for an individual to intend to reform a state by changing everything from the foundations and overturning it in order to rectify it; or even to reform the body of the sciences, or the order established in the schools to teach them; but that, as regards all the opinions that I had hitherto accepted as credible, I could not do better than to undertake to reject them once and for all and replace them afterwards by better ones, or even by the same ones, when I had [14] adjusted them to the standard of reason. And I firmly believed that by this means I would succeed in conducting my life much better than if I built only on old foundations, and relied only on the principles that I had been persuaded of in my youth, without ever having examined whether they were true. For although I noticed diverse difficulties in

---

16   Sparta was said to have received its laws from Lycurgus.

this task, they were nevertheless not without remedy, nor were they comparable to those that are found in the reformation of the least things that concern the public. Those great bodies are too difficult to raise again once torn down, or even to hold up once they have been shaken, and their fall can only be very violent. Besides, as for the imperfections they might have (which the mere diversity among them suffices to show that many do have), usage has doubtless greatly mitigated them, and has even insensibly avoided or corrected many of them, which could not have been well foreseen by prudence. Finally, they are almost always more tolerable than their alteration would be, in the same way that great roads that wind among the mountains little by little become so smooth and so comfortable from frequent use that it is much better to follow them than to try to take a straighter course by climbing over rocks and descending to the bottom of precipices.

That is why I could in no way approve those confused and restless temperaments who, being called neither by birth nor by fortune to the management of public affairs, are always thinking up some new reformation. [15] And if I thought that there was the least thing in this writing by which I could be suspected of this madness, I would be very reluctant to let it be published. My intention has never extended beyond trying to reform my own thoughts and to build on a base that is entirely my own. If, since my work has pleased me well enough, I show you here its model, it is not however because I wish to counsel anyone to imitate it. Those to whom God has better distributed his graces will perhaps have more elevated intentions, but I fear that this one is already too bold for many. The sole resolution to reject all opinions that one has formerly received as credible is not an example that each should follow, and the world is almost entirely composed of two kinds of minds for whom it is thoroughly unsuitable: namely, those who, believing themselves more competent than they are, cannot help making precipitate judgments, and lack enough patience to conduct all their thoughts in an orderly way, so that once they had taken the liberty to doubt received opinions and to depart from the common path, they would never be able to keep to the road that would take them more directly, and would remain lost all their lives; and those who, having enough reason or modesty to judge that they are less capable of distinguishing the true from the false than some others by whom they can be instructed, must be content to follow the opinions of these others, rather than seek better ones themselves.

[16] As for myself, I would no doubt have been one of the latter if I had never had but a single master, or if I had not known the differences that have existed at all times among the opinions of the most learned. But I discovered in college that one can imagine nothing so strange and

unbelievable that it has not been said by some philosopher. And later, in the course of my travels, I recognized that all those who have sentiments utterly contrary to ours are not, for that reason, barbarians or savages, but that many employ reason as much as we do, or even more. And I considered how the same man, with the same mind, if nourished from his infancy among the French or the Germans, becomes different from what he would be if he had always lived among the Chinese or the cannibals; and how even in the fashions of our dress the same thing that pleased us ten years ago, and that perhaps will please us again ten years hence, seems extravagant and ridiculous to us now. Thus it is custom and example that persuades us much more than any certain[17] knowledge, and nevertheless the preponderance of voices is not a proof worth anything as regards truths that are a little difficult to discover, because it is much more probable that a single man would have found them than a whole people. [So] I could choose no one whose opinions, it seemed to me, should be preferred to those of others, and I found myself as it were compelled to undertake to guide myself.

But like a man who walks alone and in darkness, I resolved to go so slowly and to use [17] so much circumspection in everything that, even if I advanced but a very short way, I would at least guard myself against falling. Indeed I did not wish to begin by rejecting completely any of the opinions that might previously have slipped into my beliefs without having been introduced there by reason until I had first spent enough time planning the project of the work that I would undertake, and seeking the true method of attaining the knowledge of everything of which my mind would be capable.

In my early youth I had studied, among the parts of philosophy, some logic, and in mathematics, some geometrical analysis and algebra, three arts or sciences that it seemed should contribute something to my intention.[18] But when I examined them, I observed that in the case of logic, its syllogisms and most of its other teachings are useful in explaining to others the things one knows, or even, like the art of Lully,[19] in speaking without judgment of those one does not know, rather than in learning them. And although logic indeed contains many very true and good precepts, they are mixed with so many others that are either harmful or superfluous that it is almost as difficult to separate them as it is to draw a Diana or a Minerva out of a block of marble still unshaped. As for the analysis of the ancients and the algebra of the

---

17   See Glossary, s.v. "Certain."
18   See Glossary, s.v. "Logic."
19   Raymond Lull or Lully (c. 1235-1315) was a Catalan theologian, some of whose writings were an attempt at a general art for finding truth.

moderns, aside from the fact that they extend only to matters that are very abstract and seem to be of no utility, the first is always so restricted to the consideration of figures that it cannot exercise the understanding [18] without greatly fatiguing the imagination; and in the second one is so subjected to certain rules and notations that it has been made into a confused and obscure art that encumbers the mind instead of a science that cultivates it. This was why I thought it necessary to seek some other method that comprehended the advantages of these three while being exempt from their defects. And since a multitude of laws often furnishes excuses to the vices, so that a state is much better regulated when it has only a few that are strictly observed, so instead of that great number of precepts of which logic is composed, I believed that the four following ones would be enough for me, provided that I made a firm and constant resolution never once to depart from them.[20]

The first was never to accept anything as true that I did not know evidently to be so; that is to say, carefully to avoid precipitation and prejudice, and to include nothing in my judgments except what presented itself so clearly and distinctly to my mind that I would have no occasion to place it in doubt.

The second, to divide each of the difficulties that I examined into as many parts as possible, and as would be required to resólve it better.

The third, to conduct my thoughts in order, beginning with the objects that are simplest and easiest to know, in order to ascend little by little, as by degrees, to the knowledge of the most composite, and even supposing an order among those [19] that have no natural order of precedence.

And finally, everywhere to make such complete enumerations, and such general reviews, that I would be assured of having omitted nothing.

Those long chains of reasoning, completely simple and easy, that the geometers customarily use to attain their most difficult demonstrations had given me occasion to imagine that all things that can fall under human knowledge are interconnected in the same way, and that provided only that one abstains from accepting any as true that is not, and always adheres to the order required to deduce them from one another, there cannot be any so remote that it cannot finally be reached, nor so concealed that it cannot be discovered. And I was in no great difficulty about seeking those with which it was necessary to begin; for I already knew it was with the simplest and easiest to know. And considering that of all those who have hitherto sought truth in the sciences, only the mathematicians have been able to find any demonstrations, that is,

---

20 The rules of method that follow are condensed versions of some of the rules found in Descartes's earlier *Rules for the Direction of the Native Intelligence* (1628).

certain and evident reasonings, I did not doubt that I ought to begin with the same ones they have examined, even though I expected no other utility from them except to accustom my mind to nourish itself on truths and not to content itself with false reasonings. But for that I had no intention of trying to learn all the particular sciences that are commonly called mathematics. [20] And seeing that, although their objects are different, they nevertheless agree in considering nothing but the diverse relations or proportions that are found in these objects, I thought that it would be better to examine only these proportions in general, supposing them only in subjects that would make it easier to know them, but without restricting them to those subjects, so that I could apply them better later on to all other things to which they might be suited. Then, having noted that in order to know them I would sometimes need to consider each in particular, and sometimes only to retain them, or to comprehend several together, I thought that in order to consider these proportions better in particular, I should suppose them [to hold between] lines, because I found nothing more simple or that I could represent more distinctly to my imagination and my sense; but that in order to retain them, or to comprehend many together, it was necessary to express them by certain notations, as short as possible. In this way I would borrow all the best of geometrical analysis and algebra, and correct all the defects of the one by the other.[21]

Indeed, I dare to say that the exact observation of these few precepts I have chosen gave me such facility in untangling all the questions to which these two sciences extend that in the two or three months I spent examining them, having commenced with the most simple and most general, and each truth that I found being a rule that [21] later served me to find others, I not only solved many questions that I had previously thought very difficult, but it also seemed to me toward the end that I could determine, even in those where I was ignorant, by what means and up to what point it would be possible to resolve them. In this I perhaps will not appear to you too vain, if you consider that since there is only one truth concerning each thing, whoever finds it knows as much as can be known about it, and that a child, for example, instructed in arithmetic, having made an addition according to the rules, can be assured of having found, regarding the sum, all that the human mind

---

21 Descartes in fact did combine geometrical analysis and algebra, vastly simplifying its notations, and laid out the fundamentals of analytic geometry in the *Geometry*, published along with the *Discourse* (see note 23 below). Much of the thought that underlay his account can be found in the *Rules for the Direction of the Native Intelligence*. For a study of the transformation in mathematics this accomplished, see Jacob Klein, *Greek Mathematical Thought and the Origin of Algebra*, trans. Eva Brann (Cambridge: MIT Press, 1968).

can find. For finally the method that teaches us to follow the true order, and to enumerate exactly all the particular circumstances of what we seek, contains all that gives certitude to the rules of arithmetic.

But what contented me most about this method was that by its means I was assured of using my reason in everything, if not perfectly, at least as well as was in my power. Besides which I perceived that in practicing the method my mind became accustomed little by little to conceive its objects more clearly [*nettement*] and distinctly, and since I had not restricted it to any particular matter, I promised myself to apply it as usefully to the difficulties of the other sciences as I had done to those of algebra. Not that, for that end, I dared to undertake immediately to examine all those that presented themselves, for that indeed would have been contrary to the order that it prescribed. But having taken note that their principles must all be borrowed from [22] philosophy, in which I had not yet found anything certain, I thought that I must above all try to establish such principles in it. And since this was the most important thing in the world and the one in which precipitation and bias were most to be feared, I thought that I ought not to try to carry it out until I had attained an age much more mature than the twenty-three years that I then was, and until I had employed a great deal of time in preparing myself for it, as much by uprooting from my mind all the bad opinions I had hitherto accepted as by accumulating experiments [*expériences*] that could later be the matter of my reasonings, and by always exercising myself in the method I had prescribed for myself in order to strengthen myself in it more and more.

PART 3

And finally, it is not enough, before starting to rebuild the house in which one lives, to tear it down and to provide materials and architects, or to practice architecture oneself, and in addition to have carefully drawn up the plan, but one must also be provided with another, where one can be comfortably housed while working on it. Thus in order that I might not remain irresolute in my actions while reason obliged me to be so in my judgments, and that I might continue to live henceforth as happily as I could, I formed a provisional morality[22] for myself, consisting of only three or four maxims that I would like to disclose to you.

The first was to obey the laws and customs [23] of my country, adhering constantly to the religion in which God gave me the grace

---

22 See Glossary, s.v. "Morality."

to be instructed from childhood, and governing myself in everything else according to the most moderate and least excessive opinions that were commonly received in practice among the most sensible of those with whom I would have to live. For since I had begun to count my own opinions as nothing, because I wished to submit them all to examination, I was sure that I could do no better than to follow those of the most sensible. And although there may perhaps be as sensible people among the Persians or the Chinese as among us, it seemed to me that the most useful thing was to regulate myself by those with whom I would have to live, and that in order to know what their opinions truly were, I ought to take notice of what they practiced, rather than what they said, not only because in the corruption of our morals there are few people who wish to say all that they believe, but also because many do not themselves know what they believe. For the action of thought by which one believes a thing being different from that by which one knows that one believes it, the one is often found without the other. And among several opinions equally received, I chose only the most moderate, partly because these are always the most convenient in practice and, since excess is usually bad, presumably the best, but also so that I would stray a shorter distance from the true road in case I made a mistake than I would in choosing one extreme when it was the other that should have been followed. In particular, [24] I considered as excessive all the promises by which we abandon something of our freedom. Not that I disapproved the laws that, to remedy the inconstancy of weak minds [*esprits faibles*], permit one to make vows or contracts that oblige one to persevere in them when one has some good intention or even, for the security of commerce, some intention that is merely indifferent. But because I did not see anything in the world that remained always in the same state, and because, so far as I myself was concerned, I was proposing to perfect my judgments more and more, and not to render them worse, I thought that I would commit a major violation of good sense if, because I had once approved some thing, I was obliged to consider it good after it had perhaps ceased to be so, or after I had ceased to esteem it so.

My second maxim was to be as firm and resolute in my actions as I could be, and not to follow less constantly the most doubtful opinions, when I had once determined upon them, than if they had been very assured—imitating in this regard those travelers who, finding themselves lost in some forest, must not wander now to one side, now to the other, nor still less stop in one place, but must go always as straight as they can in the same direction, and not alter it for weak reasons, although it was perhaps only chance alone at the outset that determined them to choose it. For by this means if they do not go exactly where they wish, at least they will eventually reach [25] some place where they probably will be better off than in the middle of a forest. And since the actions of life often do not permit of any delay, it is a very certain truth that when it is not in our power to discern the truest opinions, we ought to follow the most probable, and even if we do not observe that some are more probable than others, we ought nevertheless to decide on certain ones, and consider them afterwards no longer as dubious, insofar as they relate to practice, but as very true and certain, because the reason that has made us choose them is itself true and certain. And this was able henceforth to free me from all the repentance and remorse that customarily agitate the consciences of those weak and wavering minds that allow themselves the inconstancy of practicing as good the things that they afterwards judge to be bad.

My third maxim was to try always to conquer myself rather than fortune, and to change my desires rather than the order of the world, and generally to accustom myself to believe that there is nothing entirely in our power except our thoughts, so that after we have done our best regarding the things that are external to us, all that we fail to accomplish is, as far as we are concerned, absolutely impossible. And this alone seemed to me sufficient to keep me from desiring anything in the future that I might not acquire, and thus to render me content. For since our will naturally tends to [26] desire only those things that our understanding represents to it in some manner as possible, it is certain that if we consider all the goods outside of us as equally removed from our power, we will have no more regrets at lacking those that seem to be due to our birth, when we are deprived of them through no fault of our own, than we have at not possessing the kingdoms of China or Mexico; and that by making a virtue of necessity, as the saying goes, we shall no more desire to be healthy if we are sick, or to be free if we are in prison, than we now desire to have bodies made of a material as incorruptible as diamonds, or wings to fly like the birds. But I admit that it takes long practice, and often repeated meditation, to accustom oneself to look at everything from this slant, and I believe that in this mainly consisted the secret of those philosophers who were able in former times to withdraw from the empire of fortune and despite pains and poverty to rival the felicity of their gods. For by unceasing concern with the limits that were prescribed to them by nature, they persuaded themselves so perfectly that nothing was in their power but their thoughts that this alone was sufficient to prevent them from having any affection for other things, and they controlled their thoughts so absolutely that they had some reason to regard themselves as more rich, and more powerful, and more free, and more happy, than other men who, lacking this philosophy, [27] could never control everything they wanted, however favored by nature and fortune they might be.

Finally, to conclude this morality, I was drawn to make a review of the diverse occupations of men in this life in order to try to choose the best. And without wishing to say anything about those of others, I thought that I could do no better than to continue in the very one in which I found myself, that is, to spend my whole life in cultivating my reason, and to advance as much as I could in the knowledge of the truth, following the method I had prescribed for myself. I had experienced such extreme contentments since I had begun to use this method that I believed I could not obtain sweeter or more innocent ones in this life, and as I every day discovered by its means some truths that seemed to me quite important and commonly unknown to other men, the satisfaction I derived so filled my mind that nothing else affected me. Besides, the three preceding maxims were founded only on my intention to continue instructing myself. For since God has given each man some light to distinguish the true from the false, I would not have believed that I should be content with the opinions of others for a single moment if I had not proposed to use my own judgment to examine them when the time came, and I would not have been able to exempt myself from scruples in following them if I had not hoped to lose thereby no opportunity of finding better ones, if [28] there were any. And finally I would not have been able to limit my desires, or be content, if I had not followed a path by which, thinking myself assured of acquiring all the knowledge of which I was capable, I thought myself, by the same means, assured of acquiring all the true goods that would ever be in my power. For inasmuch as our will tends to pursue or avoid only those things that our understanding represents to it as good or bad, it suffices to judge well in order to do well, and to judge as best one can in order to do as best one can, that is, to acquire all the virtues together with all the other goods that one can acquire; and when one is certain that this is the case, one cannot fail to be content.

After I had thus assured myself of these maxims and had set them apart along with the truths of the faith, which have always been the first among my beliefs, I judged that I could freely undertake to rid myself of all the rest of my opinions. And since I hoped I could accomplish this better by conversing with men than by remaining longer shut up in the heated room where I had had all these thoughts, the winter was not yet over before I began once more to travel. And in all the nine following years I did nothing but roam here and there in the world, trying to be a spectator rather than an actor in all the comedies played there, and by making a particular reflection in each matter on what might make it questionable, and give us occasion for making mistakes, I meanwhile uprooted from my mind all the errors that had [29] previously slipped into it. Not that I imitated the skeptics who doubt only for the sake of doubting, and pretend to be always irresolute, for on the contrary, my whole purpose was aimed at gaining assurance, and at casting aside the shifting soil and the sand in order to find the rock or the clay. I succeeded in this well enough, it seems to me, for in trying to discover the falsity or the uncertainty of the propositions I examined, not by weak conjectures but by clear and assured reasonings, I encountered none so dubious that I could not always draw a sufficiently certain conclusion from it, even if only that it contained nothing certain. And just as in tearing down an old house one customarily salvages the old materials to use in building a new one, so in destroying all those old opinions that I judged were badly founded, I made diverse observations and acquired many experiences that have since helped me to establish more certain ones. Furthermore, I continued to practice the method I had prescribed for myself; for apart from the care I had taken generally to conduct all my thoughts according to its rules, I occasionally set aside certain hours that I used especially to practice it in mathematical problems, or even in others that I could make closely similar to mathematical ones by detaching them from all the principles of the other sciences, which I did not find sufficiently solid, as you will see I have done in several cases explained in this volume.[23] Thus without living otherwise [30] in appearance than those who, having no employment but to pass their lives in sweetness and innocence, study how to separate pleasures from vices, and who make use of every diversion that is honorable in order to enjoy their leisure without boredom, I continued to pursue my purpose, and to profit in the knowledge of the truth, perhaps more than if I had done nothing but read books or frequent men of letters.

Nevertheless, these nine years passed before I had as yet taken any stand with regard to the problems that are customarily disputed among the learned, or commenced to seek the foundations of any philosophy more certain than the ordinary. And the example of many excellent minds who had previously had such an intention, but did not seem to me to have succeeded, made me imagine it to be so difficult that I would not perhaps have dared to undertake it so soon if I had not seen that some

---

23 The *Discourse on Method* was published as an introduction to three essays: the *Dioptrics*, the *Meteors*, and the *Geometry*. Descartes claimed in a letter that his method "consists more in practice than in theory" (to Mersenne, 27 February 1637 [?]; AT 1:349) and that these essays were examples of discoveries made possible by method. In the *Dioptrics*, a work on optics, we find among other things Descartes's version of the law of refraction; in the *Geometry*, his great contribution to mathematics, analytic geometry.

had already noised it about that I had succeeded. I cannot say on what they founded that opinion, and if I contributed anything to it by my discourse, it must have been by confessing more frankly what I did not know than is customary among those who have studied a bit, and also perhaps in disclosing the reasons I had to doubt many things that others regard as certain, rather than in boasting of any doctrine. But being proud enough not to wish to be taken for other than I am, I thought that I must try by all means to make myself worthy of the reputation [31] accorded me. And it is just eight years since this desire made me resolve to leave every place in which I could have acquaintances, and to retire here, in a country where the long duration of the war has established such order that the armies maintained here seem only to enable one to enjoy the fruits of peace with the more security, and where amid the throng of a great and very active people, more concerned with their own affairs than curious about those of others, I could live as solitary and retired as in the most remote of deserts, while lacking none of the conveniences of the most populous cities.[24]

PART 4

I do not know whether I should tell you about the first meditations that I made there; for they are so metaphysical and so uncommon that they will perhaps not be to everyone's taste. Nevertheless, I find myself in some manner compelled to speak of them, in order that it may be judged whether the foundations that I have laid are sufficiently firm. I had noticed for a long time that, as regards morals, it is sometimes necessary to follow opinions that one knows to be quite uncertain just as if they were indubitable, as has been said above. But since I now desired to devote myself solely to the quest for truth, I thought it necessary that I do the very opposite, and that I reject as absolutely false everything in which I could imagine the least doubt, in order to see whether afterwards there did not remain something among my beliefs that was entirely indubitable. So, [32] because our senses sometimes deceive us, I chose to suppose that there was nothing that was such as they make us imagine it. And because there are men who make mistakes in reasoning, even about the simplest matters in geometry, and commit fallacies, judging that I was as subject to error as anyone else, I rejected as false all the reasonings that I had formerly taken as demonstrations. And finally, considering that all the same thoughts that we have while awake can come to us also while we are sleeping, without there being any that are then true,

------

24   Descartes settled in Holland in 1628 or 1629.

I resolved to feign that all the things that had ever entered my mind were not more true than the illusions of my dreams. But immediately after, I noticed that while I thus chose to think that everything was false, it was necessarily true that I, who was thinking this, was something. And observing that this truth *I think, therefore I am* was so firm and so assured that all the most extravagant suppositions of the skeptics were incapable of shaking it, I judged that I could accept it without scruple as the first principle of the philosophy that I was seeking.

Next, I examined attentively what I was, and I saw that I could feign that I had no body,[25] and that there was no world or any place where I was, but I could not feign, for all that, that I was not. On the contrary, from the very fact that I thought of doubting the truth of other things, it followed very evidently and very certainly that I was. On the other hand, if I had merely [33] ceased to think, even though all the rest of what I had ever imagined might be true, I had no reason to believe that I was. From this I knew that I was a substance whose whole essence or nature is only to think, and that does not need any place or depend on any material thing in order to be. So that this me, that is to say, the soul by which I am what I am, is entirely distinct from the body, and is even more easily known, and even if the body were not, the soul would not fail to be all that it is.

After that, I considered what in general is required for a proposition to be true and certain; for since I had just found one that I knew to be such, I thought that I should also know in what this certitude consists. And because I observed that there is nothing at all in this *I think, therefore I am* that assures me that I speak the truth except that I see very clearly that in order to think, it is necessary to be, I judged that I could take as a general rule that the things we conceive very clearly and distinctly are all true; but there is only some difficulty in observing well which those are that we conceive distinctly.

Next, reflecting on the fact that I was doubting, and that consequently my being was not wholly perfect (for I saw clearly that it was a greater perfection to know than to doubt), I was drawn to inquire whence I had learned to think of something more perfect than I was. And I recognized it as evident that this must be [34] from some nature that was in fact more perfect. As regards the thoughts that I had of many other things outside of me, like the sky, the earth, light, heat, and a thousand others, I did not have so much difficulty in knowing whence they came, because not observing anything in them that seemed to make them superior to me, I could believe that if they were true, they depended on my nature,

---

25 See Glossary, s.v. "Body."

insofar as it had some perfection; and that if they were not, I got them from nothing, that is, they were in me because I had some defect. But it could not be the same with the idea of a being more perfect than mine; for to have gotten it from nothing was a thing manifestly impossible, and because it is no less contradictory that the more perfect should follow from and depend on the less perfect than that something should proceed from nothing, I could not have gotten it from myself either. So that what remained was that it had been put in me by a nature that was truly more perfect than I was, and that even had in itself all the perfections of which I could have any idea, that is to say, to explain myself in a word, that was God. To which I added that since I knew some perfections that I did not have, I was not the only being that existed (I will use freely here, if you please, the words of the School), but that there had of necessity to be some other more perfect being on which I depended, and from which I had acquired all that I have. For had I been alone and independent of everything else, so that I had gotten [35] from myself the little by which I participated in the perfect being, I could have gotten from myself, by the same argument, all the remainder that I knew I lacked, and so been myself infinite, eternal, immutable, all-knowing, all-powerful, and in short could have had all the perfections that I could discern to be in God.[26] For according to the reasonings I have just used, in order to know the nature of God, so far as my nature was capable of it, I had only to consider, as regards all the things of which I found in myself some idea, whether it was a perfection or not to possess them. And I was sure that none of those that showed some imperfection were in him, but that all the others were. Thus I saw that doubt, inconstancy, sadness, and the like could not be in him, since I myself would have liked to be rid of them. Further, I had ideas of many sensible and corporeal things; for although I supposed that I dreamed, and that all that I saw or imagined was false, nevertheless I could not deny that these ideas were truly in my thought. But because I had already recognized very clearly that in me the intelligent nature is distinct from the corporeal, and considering that all composition is a sign of dependence, and that dependence is manifestly a defect, I judged that it could not be a perfection in God to be composed of these two natures, and that consequently he was not. But if there were some bodies in the world, or even some intelligences or other natures that were not wholly [36] perfect, their being must depend on his power, so that they could not subsist without him a single moment.

After this I wished to seek for other truths, and representing to myself the object of the geometers, which I conceived as a continuous

---

26   These are perfections attributed to God in Christian theology.

body, or a space indefinitely extended in length, breadth, and height or depth, divisible into different parts, which could have different figures or magnitudes, and be moved or transposed in all sorts of ways—for the geometers suppose all this in their object—I went through some of their simpler demonstrations.[27] And having taken note that this great certainty that everyone attributes to them is founded only on the fact that they are conceived evidently, according to the rule mentioned above, I also took note that there was nothing at all in them that assured me of the existence of their object. For example, I saw quite well that if we suppose a triangle, it was necessary that its three angles be equal to two right angles; but for all that I saw nothing that assured me that there was any triangle in the world. On the other hand, going back to examine the idea I had of a perfect being, I found that existence was contained in it in the same way as in the idea of a triangle is contained the equality of its three angles to two right angles, or in the idea of a sphere the equidistance of all its parts from its center, or even more evidently. Consequently it is at least as certain that God, who is this perfect being, is or exists, as any demonstration in geometry can be.[28]

[37] But that which causes many to be persuaded that it is difficult to know God, and even to know what their soul is, is that they never elevate their mind above sensible things, and that they are so accustomed to consider nothing except by imagining it—a mode of thinking peculiar to material things—that whatever is not imaginable seems to them unintelligible. This is clear enough even from the maxim held by the philosophers in the schools that there is nothing in the understanding that has not first been in the senses, where nevertheless it is certain that the ideas of God and the soul have never been. And it seems to me that those who want to use their imagination in order to understand them do just the same as if they wanted to use their eyes to hear sounds or smell odors, except that there is also this difference, that the sense of sight assures us no less of the truth of its objects than do those of smell or hearing, whereas neither our imagination nor our senses can ever assure us of anything without the aid of our understanding.

---

27   As early as the *Rules for the Direction of the Native Intelligence* Descartes tells us that arithmetic and geometry are more certain than other disciplines because the object with which they deal is "so pure and simple" that one need rely on no assumptions from experience, which may introduce uncertainty. This object, which he characterizes here in the *Discourse* as "a space indefinitely extended in length, breadth, and height…divisible into different parts," allows him to think about matter as intelligible (see *The World, or Treatise on Light* [1629-33]).

28   This is the Cartesian version of what is called the ontological argument for the existence of God, which we find in the *Proslogion* of St. Anselm of Canterbury (1033-1109).

Finally, if there still are men who are not sufficiently persuaded of the existence of God and of their soul by the reasons I have offered, I would have them know that all other things of which they perhaps think they are more sure—such as having a body, and that there are stars and an earth, and the like—are less certain. For while we have a moral assurance[29] of these things that is such that it seems [38] extravagant to doubt them, nevertheless when it is a question of metaphysical certitude we cannot reasonably deny that there is reason enough not to be entirely sure of them, when we take note that we can in the same way imagine when asleep that we have another body, and that we see other stars, and another earth, without any of this being so. For how do we know that the thoughts that come in dreams are more false than others, since often they are not less vivid and positive? Let the best minds study this as much as they like, I do not believe that they can give a sufficient reason to remove this doubt unless they presuppose the existence of God. For in the first place, the very thing that I just now took as a rule, namely, that the things that we conceive very clearly and very distinctly are all true, is sure only because God is or exists, and is a perfect being, and all that is in us comes from him. It follows that our ideas or notions, being real things, and proceeding from God, cannot fail to be true insofar as they are clear and distinct. So that if we often enough have some that contain falsity, it can only be from those that have something confused and obscure about them, because in this regard they participate in nothing, that is to say, they are thus confused in us because we are not wholly perfect. For it is evident that it is no less contradictory that falsity or imperfection [39] as such should proceed from God than that truth or perfection should proceed from nothing. But if we did not know that all that is real and true in us comes from a perfect and infinite being, we would have no reason to assure us that our ideas had the perfection of being true, no matter how clear and distinct[30] they were.

But after the knowledge of God and the soul have thus made us certain of this rule, it is quite easy to know that the dreams that we imagine while asleep must not make us doubt in any way the truth of the thoughts that we have while awake. For if it happened, even while dreaming, that someone had some very distinct idea, as, for example, that a geometer invented some new demonstration, his being asleep would not prevent it from being true. And as regards the most ordinary error of our dreams, which is that they represent to us various objects in the same way as do our external senses, it does not matter that it supplies an occasion to distrust the truth of such ideas, because they can

---

29   See Glossary, s.v. "Certain."
30   See Glossary, s.v. "Clear and Distinct (Ideas)."

also deceive us often enough when we are not sleeping, as when those who have jaundice see everything colored yellow, or when the stars or other very remote bodies appear to us much smaller than they are. For finally, whether we are awake or whether we sleep, we ought never let ourselves be persuaded except by the evidence of our reason. And it should be noted that I say by our reason, and not by our imagination or our senses. For although we see the sun [40] very clearly, we must not therefore judge that it is only of the size that we see it to be; and we can indeed distinctly imagine a lion's head grafted onto a goat's body, without therefore having to conclude that there is a chimera[31] in the world. For reason does not dictate to us that what we thus see or imagine is true. But it indeed dictates to us that all our ideas or notions must have some foundation of truth; for it would be impossible that God, who is wholly perfect and wholly truthful, would have put them in us without that. And because our reasonings are never so evident or complete during sleep as during wakefulness, although sometimes our imaginings are then just as vivid and positive or more so, it dictates to us too that although our thoughts cannot all be true, because we are not wholly perfect, what they have of truth must infallibly be met with in those we have when awake rather than in our dreams.

Part 5

I would be very glad to continue, and to show here the whole chain of other truths that I have deduced from these first ones. But because to do that it would now be necessary that I speak of several questions that are controversial among the learned, with whom I do not desire to be embroiled, I believe that it will be better that I abstain, and only say in general what they are, in order to let the wisest judge whether it would be useful that the public be more particularly informed of them. I have [41] always remained firm in the resolution I have made to assume no other principle than that which I have just used to demonstrate the existence of God and the soul, and to accept nothing as true that did not seem to me to be more clear and certain than the demonstrations of the geometers had formerly seemed. Nevertheless, I dare to say that not only have I found a way to satisfy myself in a short time concerning the principal difficulties usually dealt with in philosophy, but I have also discerned certain laws that God has so established in nature, and of which he has imprinted such notions in our souls, that after sufficient

---

31   In Greek mythology, a fire-breathing she-monster, usually represented as a com-
     posite of a lion, goat, and serpent.

reflection, we cannot doubt that they are exactly observed in all that is or happens in the world. Moreover, on considering the consequences of these laws, I seem to have discovered many truths more useful and more important than all that I had previously learned, or even hoped to learn.

But because I have tried to explain the principal ones in a treatise that certain considerations prevent me from publishing,[32] I cannot better make them known than by summarizing here what it contains. I had intended to include all that I thought I knew, before writing it, about the nature of material things. But just as painters who cannot represent equally well on a picture plane all the different faces of a solid body choose a principal one to put in the light and leave the [42] others in shadow, making them appear only to the extent that they can be seen while looking at the principal one, so because I feared that I could not put in my discourse all that I had in my thought, I attempted to expose fully there only what I had conceived about light. I then took the occasion to add something about the sun and the fixed stars because almost all of it comes from them; about the heavens because they transmit it; about the planets, the comets, and the earth because they cause its reflection; and in particular about all the bodies on the earth because they are colored, or transparent, or luminous; and finally about man because he is the spectator of it. But to leave all these things somewhat in shadow, and to be able to say more freely what I judged of them without being obliged either to follow or to refute the opinions received by the learned, I resolved to leave all this present world to their disputes, and to speak only of what would happen in a new world if God now created somewhere in imaginary spaces enough matter to compose it and agitated the different parts of this matter in different ways and without order, so that he made of it a chaos as confused as the poets could feign, and afterwards did nothing but lend his ordinary assent to nature, and let it act according to the laws that he established. Hence I first described this matter, and tried to represent it so that there is nothing in the world, it seems to me, more clear or intelligible, except what has been said just now of God and the soul; for I even assumed, explicitly, that [43] there were in it none of those forms or qualities about which one disputes in the schools, or in general anything whose knowledge was not so natural to our souls that one could not even feign to be ignorant of it. In addition I showed what

---

32   This treatise, *The World, or Treatise on Light*, was written during 1629-33. In the opening paragraph of Part 6 below Descartes reveals that he is thinking about the condemnation of Galileo Galilei (1564-1642) by the Roman Catholic Church for publishing his defense of Copernicanism, the theory that the sun is the center around which the earth and other planets revolve. In *The World* Descartes's account of creation is one that is avowedly hypothetical, as he reports below.

the laws of nature were, and without basing my reasonings on any other principle than the infinite perfections of God, I tried to demonstrate all those of which one could have some doubt, and to show that they are such that even if God had created several worlds, there could not be any in which they failed to be observed. After that I showed how as a consequence of these laws most of the matter of this chaos had to dispose and arrange itself in a certain manner that rendered it similar to our heavens; how, meanwhile, some of its parts had to form an earth, and some planets and comets, and others a sun and fixed stars. Here, enlarging on the subject of light, I explained at some length what sort had to be found in the sun and the stars, and how from there it traversed in an instant the immense spaces of the heavens, and how it was reflected from the planets and comets towards the earth. I also added several things regarding the substance, situation, movements, and all the diverse qualities of these heavens and these stars, so that I thought that I said enough about it to make known that nothing is observed in the heavens and stars of this world that should not, or at least could not, appear entirely similar in those of the world [44] I described. Thence I came to speak of the earth in particular: how, although I had explicitly assumed that God had put no weight whatever in the matter of which it was constituted, all its parts did not fail to tend exactly towards its center; how, since it had water and air on its surface, the disposition of the heavens and the stars, but mainly of the moon, had to cause an ebb and flow that was similar, in all its circumstances, to what is observed in our oceans, and in addition to that a certain current, of water as much as of air, from east to west, as is observed among the tropics; how the mountains, the oceans, the springs, and the rivers could be formed there naturally, and the metals come to be in the mines, and the plants to grow in the fields, and how in general all the bodies that one calls mixed or composite could be engendered. And among other things, because apart from the stars I know nothing in the world that produces light besides fire, I made it my study to make understood quite clearly all that belongs to its nature, how it occurs and how it is fed; how it has sometimes only heat without light, and sometimes only light without heat; how it can induce different colors in different bodies, and different other qualities; how it melts some of them and hardens others; how it can consume almost all of them or convert them into ashes and smoke; and finally, how from these ashes, by the violence alone of its action, it forms glass: for since this transmutation of [45] ashes into glass seems to me as wonderful as any other that happens in nature, I took particular pleasure in describing it.

Nevertheless, I did not want to infer from all these things that this world has been created in the manner that I proposed, for it is indeed more probable that God has made it from the beginning such as it was to be. But it is certain, and it is an opinion commonly received among the theologians, that the action by which he now conserves it is entirely the same as that by which he has created it;[33] so that although he had not given it, at the beginning, any other form than chaos, provided that having established the laws of nature he lent to it his assent to act as it customarily does, we can believe, without doing injury to the miracle of creation, that by that means alone all the things that are purely material could have rendered themselves in time such as we see them at present. And their nature is much easier to conceive when we see them begin to grow little by little in this way than when we only consider them as fully complete.

From the description of inanimate bodies and plants I passed on to that of animals and particularly to that of men. But because I did not yet have enough knowledge to speak of them in the same style as of the rest, that is, demonstrating effects by causes, and showing from what seeds, and in what manner, nature must produce them, I contented myself with assuming that God formed the body of a man entirely similarly to [46] one of ours, in the exterior shape of its members as much as in the interior conformation of its organs, without composing it from other matter than that I had described, and without putting into it, at the beginning, any reasonable soul, or any other thing to serve as a vegetative or sensitive soul, except that he ignited in its heart one of those fires without light that I had already explained, and that I did not conceive as of a different nature from that which heats hay when we have gathered it before it is dry or which makes new wines bubble when we let them ferment over the crushed grapes. For examining the functions that such a body could consequently have, I found precisely all those that can be in us without our thinking, and hence without our soul—that is to say, that part distinct from the body whose nature is only to think, as said above—contributing to them, and that are all the very ones in which we can say that animals without reason resemble us. But I was not for all that able to find any of those that depend on thought and hence are the only ones that belong to us as men, whereas I found them all afterwards when I assumed that God created a reasonable soul and joined it to this body in a certain way that I described.

But in order to show in what way I treated this matter, I wish to

---

33   Descartes calls on the Scholastic theological idea according to which the conservation of the world does not require further creative acts by God but is part of the act of creation itself.

insert here the explanation of the movement of the heart and arteries; since it is the first and most general that we observe in animals, one will easily judge from it what one should [47] think of all the others. And so that they will have less difficulty in understanding what I will say, I would like those who are not versed in anatomy to take the pains, before reading this, to have cut up in front of them the heart of some large animal that has lungs, for it is in everything sufficiently like that of man, and let them observe the two chambers or cavities there. First, there is that in its right side, to which two very large tubes are connected, namely, the vena cava, which is the principal receptacle of the blood, and like the trunk of a tree of which the other veins of the body are the branches; and the arterial vein, which has been badly named, because it is in fact an artery that takes its origin in the heart and divides after leaving it into many branches that proceed to spread throughout the lungs. Next, that which is in the left side, to which are connected in the same way two tubes, which are as large or larger than the preceding, namely, the venous artery, which has also been badly named, because it is nothing but a vein that comes from the lungs, where it divides into many branches, interlaced with those of the arterial vein and those of that passage called the windpipe, where the air we breathe enters; and the great artery, which, after leaving the heart, sends its branches throughout the body.[34] I would also like them to be carefully shown the eleven little membranes like so many little doors that open and close the four entrances of these two cavities: [48] namely, three at the entry to the vena cava, where they are so arranged that they cannot prevent the blood it contains from flowing into the right cavity of the heart, but nevertheless effectively prevent it from being able to leave it; three at the entry to the arterial vein, which, being arranged in the opposite manner, permit the blood in this cavity to pass into the lungs, but not that which is in the lungs to return; then, two others at the entry of the venous artery, which let the blood from the lungs flow towards the left cavity of the heart, but prevent its return; and three at the entry to the great artery, which permit it to leave the heart, but prevent it from returning there. And there is no need to seek any other reason for the number of these membranes than that the opening of the venous artery, being oval because of its location, can conveniently be closed with two, whereas the others, being round, can better be closed with three. I would like them to consider, moreover, that the great artery and arterial vein are of a far firmer and harder composition than the venous artery and the vena cava; and that the latter two broaden before entering the heart,

---

34 What Descartes calls the arterial vein and the venous artery are now called the pulmonary artery and the pulmonary vein respectively.

where they form two pouches called the auricles composed of flesh like its own; and that there is always more heat in the heart than in any other place in the body; and finally, that this heat is capable of making any drop of blood that enters its cavities promptly expand and [49] dilate, just as all liquids generally do when we let them fall drop by drop into some very hot vessel.

For, after that is said, I need only add in order to explain the movement of the heart that when its cavities are not full of blood, it flows there necessarily from the vena cava into the right, and from the venous artery into the left, since these two vessels are always full of blood, and their openings, which face the heart, cannot then be blocked; but that as soon as two drops of blood have entered, one in each cavity, these drops, which must be very large because the openings by which they enter are very large and the vessels from which they come very full of blood, become rarified and dilated because of the heat that they find there, by means of which they expand the whole heart, and push and close the five little doors that are at the entries of the two vessels from which they came, preventing any more blood from descending to the heart; and continuing to rarefy more and more, they push and open the six other little doors, which are at the entries of the two other vessels by which they leave, thus causing the branches of the arterial vein and the great artery to expand almost at the same instant as the heart, which immediately afterwards contracts as the arteries also do, because the blood that has entered there cools, and their six little doors close, and the five of the vena cava and venous artery reopen, and give passage to [50] two other drops of blood, which again expand the heart and the arteries, just as before. And because the blood that thus enters the heart passes through the two pouches that are called the auricles, their movement is contrary to its own and they contract when the heart expands. Moreover, so that those who do not know the force of mathematical demonstrations and are not accustomed to distinguish true from probable reasons will not attempt to deny this without examination, I would like to inform them that the movement that I have just explained follows as necessarily from the disposition alone of the organs that can be seen in the heart with the naked eye, and from the heat that can be felt there with the fingers, and from the nature of the blood that can be known by experience, as does the movement of a clock from the force, arrangement, and shape of its counterweights and wheels.

But if one should ask why the blood from the veins is never exhausted while flowing continuously into the heart, and why the arteries are never too full, since all that passes through the heart goes into them, I need only reply what has already been written by a physician of England,[35] who must be praised for having broken the ice on this subject, and for being the first to teach that at the extremities of the arteries there are many small passages by which the blood that they receive from the heart enters into the little branches of the veins, from which they go back to the heart, so that its course is only a [51] perpetual circulation. He proves this very well by the ordinary experience of surgeons who, having bound an arm fairly tightly above the place where they have opened a vein, cause the blood to flow out more abundantly than if they had not bound it at all. And the opposite happens if they have bound it below, between the hand and the opening, or even if they have bound it very tightly above. For it is obvious that a moderately tight binding, which can prevent the blood that is already in the arm from returning to the heart by the veins, cannot thereby prevent fresh blood from coming there by means of the arteries, because they are situated beneath the veins, and their membranes are harder and less easy to press, and also because the blood that comes from the heart tends to pass through the arteries to the hand with more force than it does in returning from there to the heart by the veins. And since this blood flows out from the arm through an opening in the veins, there must necessarily be some passages below the binding, namely, towards the extremities of the arm, through which it can flow from the arteries. He also proves very well what he says about the course of the blood by certain small membranes so arranged in different places along the length of the veins that they do not permit the blood to pass from the middle of the body to the extremities but only to return from the extremities to the heart, and further, by an experiment that shows that all the blood in the body can leave in a short time by a single artery, even though it be tightly bound near the heart, if it is cut between the binding and the heart, so that there [52] is no reason to imagine that the blood that flows out comes from elsewhere.

But there are several other things that testify that the true cause of this movement of the blood is what I have said. First of all, the difference that is noticed between the blood that comes from the veins and that which comes from the arteries can only derive from its being rarefied and distilled, as it were, in passing through the heart, and hence being finer, livelier, and warmer immediately after it leaves, that is, when it is in the arteries, than it is shortly before entering the heart, that is, when it is in the veins. And if one observes carefully it will be found that this

---

35   William Harvey (1578-1657) published his discovery of the circulation of the blood in the treatise *On the Movement of the Heart and Blood in Animals* in 1628. The text has the marginal notation "Hervaeus, *de motu cordis*," identifying Harvey and his treatise.

difference is very apparent only near the heart, and not nearly as much at places farther away. Besides, the hardness of the membranes of which the arterial vein and the great artery are composed shows sufficiently that the blood beats against them with greater force than against the veins. And why should the left cavity of the heart and the great artery be broader and larger than the right cavity and the arterial vein? It must be because the blood from the venous artery, having only been in the lungs since it has passed through the heart, is thinner and rarefies more fully and easily than that which comes immediately from the vena cava. And what could physicians learn when they take our pulse if they did not know that as the nature of the blood changes, it can be rarefied by the heat of the heart to a greater or lesser extent, and with more or less rapidity, than before? And if we inquire how this heat is transmitted to the other members, must we not admit that it is [53] by means of the blood that is reheated as it passes through the heart and spreads from there throughout the body? Hence if the blood is taken away from some part, the heat is taken away by the same means, and even if the heart were as hot as molten iron it would not suffice to warm the feet and hands as much as it does by continually sending them new blood. And we therefore know too that the true utility of breathing is to carry enough fresh air into the lungs to cause the blood that comes there from the right cavity of the heart, where it has been rarefied and changed into vapors, as it were, to thicken and become converted into blood again before returning to the left cavity, for otherwise it would not be fit to serve as fuel for the fire in the heart. This is confirmed by the fact that animals without lungs have only one cavity in their hearts, and that infants in the womb, who cannot use their lungs, have an opening through which blood flows from the vena cava into the left cavity of the heart, and a passage by which it flows from the arterial vein into the great artery, without passing through the lungs. And how could digestion take place in the stomach if the heart did not send heat there through the arteries, along with some of the most fluid parts of the blood, which help to dissolve the foods put there? And is it not easy to understand the action that converts the juice of these foods into blood if we consider that it is distilled in passing and repassing through the heart perhaps more than one or two hundred times a day? And what else is needed [54] to explain nutrition and the production of the various humors of the body except that the force with which the blood, as it becomes rarefied, flows from the heart toward the extremities of the arteries causes some of its parts to stop in certain members and to take the place of others that they drive out, and that according to the situation, or shape, or smallness of the pores they encounter, some go to certain places rather than to others, just as anyone can have seen different sorts of grain being sorted out by using sieves with holes of different sizes? Finally, what is most remarkable in all of this is the generation of the animal spirits, which are like a very subtle wind, or rather like a very pure and lively flame that, constantly rising in great abundance from the heart to the brain, goes from there through the nerves to the muscles, and gives movement to all the members.[36] We need imagine no other cause of the parts of the blood that, being most agitated and most penetrating, are the best fitted to constitute these spirits going to the brain rather than elsewhere than that the arteries proceed from the heart to the brain in the straightest line of all, and that according to the rules of mechanics, which are the same as those of nature, whenever a number of things tend to move together towards the same place where there is not room for all, just as the parts of the blood that come from the left cavity of the heart tend towards the brain, [55] the weaker and less agitated ones must be turned aside by the stronger, so that only the latter arrive.

I had explained all these things in sufficient detail in the treatise I had previously intended to publish. And next I had shown what the structure of the nerves and the muscles of the human body must be so that the animal spirits within it might have the force to move its members, just as we see heads still moving and biting the earth just after they have been cut off, even though they are no longer animate. I then showed what changes must take place in the brain in order to cause waking, sleep, and dreams; how light, sounds, odors, tastes, heat, and all the other qualities of external objects can imprint on the brain various ideas by means of the senses; how hunger, thirst, and other internal passions can also send there their ideas; what must be understood as the common sense, where these ideas are received; as the memory, which conserves them; and as the imagination, which can change them in various ways and compose new ideas from them, and by this very means, distributing animal spirits to the muscles, make the members of this body move in as many different ways, according to the objects that are presented to its senses and the internal passions that are in it, as our bodies can move without the will directing them. This will not seem at all strange to those who, knowing how many different *automata*, or moving machines, can be made by human ingenuity [56] without using a great number of parts, in comparison with the great multitude of bones, muscles, nerves, arteries, veins, and all other parts that are found in the bodies of each animal, will consider this body as a machine that, having been made by the hands of God, is incomparably better

---

36   Animal spirits (*esprits animaux*) in Descartes's account are very fine, fast-moving
       material particles.

ordered, and has in itself more admirable movements, than any that can be invented by men.[37]

And I halted here particularly to show that if there were such machines as had the organs and the shape of an ape, or some other animal without reason, we would have no way of recognizing that they were not in every way of the same nature as these animals; whereas if there were machines that resembled our bodies and imitated our actions as much as is morally possible, we would always have two very certain means of recognizing that they were not for all that true men. The first is that they could never use words or other signs by putting them together as we do in order to declare our thoughts to others. For we can indeed conceive of a machine so made that it utters words, and even that it utters words in connection with bodily actions that will cause some change in its organs—for example, if we touch it in a certain spot, it asks what we want to say to it, and if in another, it cries out that we are hurting it, and the like—but not that it arranges words in different ways to [57] reply to the meaning of all that is said in its presence, as even the dullest men can do. And secondly, although they might do many things as well or even better than any of us, they would inevitably fail in some others, so that we would discover that they acted not from knowledge but only according to the arrangement of their organs. For whereas reason is a universal instrument that can serve in all sorts of encounters, these organs need some particular arrangement for each particular action; hence it is morally impossible for there to be enough different arrangements in one machine to make it act in all the circumstances of life in the same way that our reason makes us act.

Now by these same two means can be known too the difference between men and beasts. For it is a very remarkable thing that there are no men so dull and so stupid, not even madmen, that they are incapable of arranging various words together and composing from them a discourse by which they make their thoughts understood, while on the contrary there is no other animal, no matter how perfect and how fortunately born it may be, that can do the like. This is not due to a lack of organs, for we see that magpies and parrots can utter words just as we do, and nevertheless cannot speak as we do, namely, by showing that they think what they say; whereas men who are born deaf and dumb and are deprived of the organs others use [58] to speak with as much or more than beasts customarily invent by themselves certain signs by which they make themselves understood to those who are ordinarily with them and have the leisure to learn their language. And this shows

---

37   Descartes elaborates more on animals as machines in his correspondence with Henry More. See, for example, 5 February 1649 (AT 5:275-79).

not only that beasts have less reason than men, but that they have none at all. For we see that very little is required to be able to speak; and since we observe that there is as much inequality among animals of the same species as there is among men, and that some are easier to train than others, it is not credible that an ape or a parrot that is one of the most perfect of its species should not be able to equal in this respect the most stupid child, or at least a child who had a defective brain, if their soul were not of a wholly different nature from ours. And we must not confuse words with natural movements that indicate the passions and can be imitated by machines as well as by animals, or think, like certain ancients, that beasts speak, although we do not understand their language; for if that were true, since they have many organs that correspond to ours, they could make themselves as well understood by us as by their own kind. It is also quite remarkable that although there are many animals that show more ingenuity than us in some of their actions, we see nevertheless that the same ones show none at all in many others, so that what they do better than we does not prove that they have any mind—for in that case they would have more than any of us and [59] do better in everything—but rather that they have none at all, and that it is nature that acts in them according to the arrangement of their organs. In the same way we see that a clock, which is composed only of gears and springs, can count the hours and measure time more exactly than we can with all our prudence.

I had described, after that, the rational soul, and showed that it cannot be drawn in any way from the power of matter, like the other things of which I had spoken, but that it must be expressly created. And I showed how it is not sufficient that it be lodged in the human body like a pilot in his ship, except perhaps in order to move its members, but that it must be more closely joined and united with it for it to have in addition sentiments and appetites similar to ours, and so to compose a true man. Moreover, I dwelt a little on the subject of the soul because it is one of the most important. For, after the error of those who deny God, which I think I have sufficiently refuted above, there is none that leads weak minds further from the strict path of virtue than to imagine that the soul of beasts is of the same nature as ours, and that consequently we have nothing to fear or to hope for after this life, any more than the flies and the ants. But when we know how much they differ, we comprehend much better the reasons that prove that our soul is of a nature entirely independent of the body, and consequently that it is not subject to dying with it; then, inasmuch [60] as we see no other causes that destroy it, we are naturally led thereby to judge that it is immortal.

PART 6

It is now three years since I completed the treatise that contains all these things, and began to review it before putting it in the hands of the printer, when I learned that certain persons to whom I defer, and whose authority over my actions can scarcely be less than that of my own reason over my thoughts, had disapproved of a certain opinion in physics,[38] published shortly before by someone else.[39] I do not wish to say that I agreed with it, but since I had noticed nothing in it before their censure that I could imagine to be prejudicial either to religion or to the state, or consequently that would have prevented me from writing it if reason had so persuaded me, this made me fear that there might nevertheless be found among my thoughts some one that was mistaken, despite the great care I have always taken not to receive new ones among my beliefs of which I did not have very certain demonstrations, and to write nothing that could turn to the disadvantage of anyone. This sufficed to compel me to change the resolution that I had made to publish them. For although the reasons for which I had previously made it were very strong, my inclination, which had always made me hate the trade of producing books, immediately made me find enough other reasons to excuse me from it. And these reasons on both sides of the matter are such that not [61] only do I have some interest in stating them here, but perhaps the public will also have some interest in knowing them.

I have never made much of the things that came from my mind, and so long as the only fruits I gathered from the method I use were in satisfying myself regarding certain difficulties that belong to the speculative sciences or in trying to regulate my morals by the reasons that it taught me, I did not believe that I was obliged to write anything about it. For with regard to morals, everyone is so impressed with his own judgment that there would be found as many reformers as heads if others besides those whom God has established as sovereigns over his peoples, or to whom he has given enough grace and zeal to be prophets, were permitted to try to change anything in them. And although my speculations pleased me greatly, I believed that others also had some that pleased them perhaps more. But as soon as I had acquired certain general notions about physics, and after beginning to test them on various particular questions had noticed where they might lead, and

---

38 See Glossary, s.v. "Physics."
39 Galileo's *Dialogue Concerning the Two Chief World Systems* (1632) was placed on the Index of Prohibited Books by the Congregation of the Holy Office of the Roman Catholic Church in 1633 (see note 32 above).

how much they differ from the principles in use up to the present, I believed that I could not keep them hidden without gravely sinning against the law that obliges us to procure, so much as we can, the general good of all men. For they have shown me that it is possible to attain knowledge that is very useful to life, and that in place of that speculative philosophy that is taught in the schools, we can find [62] a practical one, by which, because it knows the force and actions of fire, water, air, stars, the heavens, and all the other bodies that surround us as distinctly as we know the different trades of our artisans, we could employ them in the same way in all their proper uses, and thus make ourselves like masters and possessors of nature. [40] This is desirable not only for the invention of an infinity of artifices that would enable us to enjoy, without any pain, the fruits of the earth and all the goods to be found there, but also and principally for the conservation of health, which is without doubt the primary good and the foundation of all other goods of this life. For even the mind is so dependent on the temperament and on the arrangement of the organs of the body that, if it is possible to find some means that generally renders men more wise and more capable than they have been up to now, I believe that we must seek for it in medicine. It is true that the medicine now practiced contains little whose utility is so remarkable, but although I have no intention of deprecating it, I am sure that there is nobody, even among those who make a profession of it, who does not admit that all we now know is almost nothing in comparison with what remains to be known, and that we could be spared an infinity of diseases, of the body as well as of the mind, and even also perhaps the enfeeblement of old age, if we had enough knowledge of their causes and of all the remedies that nature has provided us. And because I intended [63] to use my whole life in the search for so necessary a science, and had found a path by following which it seemed to me that one must infallibly find it, unless prevented by the brevity of life or the lack of experiments [*expériences*], I judged that there was no better remedy against these two impediments than to communicate faithfully to the public all the little that I had found, and to urge good minds to try to go further by contributing, each according to his inclination and

---

40 The project of mastery of nature is notably anticipated by Francis Bacon (1561-1626) in the *Great Instauration* and *New Organon* of 1620; see especially *New Organon* 1.129, where Bacon speaks of establishing and extending "the power and domin-ion of the human race itself over the universe" (*Selected Philosophical Works*, ed. Rose-Mary Sargent [Indianapolis: Hackett, 1999], 147). André Lalande arranges passages from Bacon and Descartes's *Discourse* side by side in "Some Texts of Bacon and Descartes," *The St. John's Review* 43/3 (1996): 51-75 (originally published as "Quelques textes de Bacon et de Descartes," *Revue de métaphysique et de morale* 19 [1911]: 296-311).

power, to the experiments required, and also by communicating to the
public everything that they learned, in order that later inquirers might
begin where their predecessors had arrived. Thus we all together might
go much further, joining the lives and labors of many, than each in
particular could.

I also noted, with regard to experiments, that they are all the more
necessary as one's knowledge is more advanced. For in the beginning
it is better to use only those that present themselves to our senses,
and of which we cannot be ignorant provided we make the slightest
reflection whatever, rather than to seek for those that are more rare and
elaborate. The reason for this is that the more rare often deceive when
we do not yet know the more general causes, and the circumstances on
which they depend are almost always so particular and so small that it
is very difficult to discern them. But the order that I have maintained
in this is the following. First, I have tried to find in general the [64]
principles or first causes of all that is, or can be, in the world, without
considering, for this purpose, anything but God alone, who has created
it, or deriving them elsewhere than from certain seeds of truth that are
naturally in our souls. After this, I examined which were the first and
most ordinary effects that can be deduced from these causes. And in so
doing, it seemed to me, I found the heavens, stars, an earth, and even, on
the earth, water, air, fire, minerals, and other such things that are most
general of all and most simple, and consequently the easiest to know.
Then, when I sought to descend to those that were more particular, so
many different ones presented themselves to me that I did not believe
it possible for the human mind to distinguish the forms or species of
bodies on the earth from an infinity of others that could be there, if it
had been the will of God to put them there, or consequently to make
them useful to us, unless we seek causes from effects, and make use
of many particular experiments. Consequently, when my mind goes
over all the objects that were ever presented to my senses, I dare to say
that I have noticed nothing that I could not conveniently explain by the
principles that I had found. But I must also admit that the power of
nature is so plentiful and vast, and these principles are so simple and
general, that I notice almost no particular effect that I do not at the
outset recognize can [65] be deduced from them in several different
ways, and my greatest difficulty is ordinarily to find in which of these
ways it depends on them. For this I know no other expedient but again to
seek more experiments that are such that their result cannot be the same
if it must be explained in one way rather than another. Moreover, I am
now at the point where, it seems to me, I see well enough what approach
must be taken to make most of those that can serve this purpose. But I

also see that they are of such kind, and so many in number, that neither my hands nor my income, even if I had a thousand times more than I do, would suffice for them all. So that to the degree that I henceforth have the capacity to make more or less of them, I shall also advance more or less in the knowledge of nature. This was what I promised to make known through the treatise I had written, and to show there so clearly the utility that the public can obtain from it that I would oblige all those who desire in general the good of men, that is to say, all those who are in fact virtuous and do not falsely seem so, to communicate to me the experiments they have already made, as well as to help me in the search for those that remain to be made.

But I have had, since that time, other reasons that have made me change my opinion and think that I ought really to go on writing all the things that I judged to be of some importance, so far as I discovered the truth about them, and to devote to them the same care as if I wished to print them, [66] so as to have all the more opportunity to examine them well, since we doubtless always look more carefully at what we believe will be seen by others than at what we only do for ourselves, and often the things that have seemed true to me when I started to conceive them have appeared false when I sought to put them on paper. Also, I did not want to lose any occasion to benefit the public, if I am capable of doing so; and if my writings are of some worth, those who will have them after my death may so use them as will seem appropriate. But I thought that I should in no way consent for them to be published during my life, so that neither the opposition and controversy to which they would perhaps be subject nor even such reputation as they could gain me should occasion any loss of the time I intended to use to instruct myself. For although it is true that each man is obliged to procure, as much as is in him, the good of others, and that to be useful to nobody is strictly to be worth nothing, it is nevertheless also true that our cares must extend beyond the present time, and that it is good to omit the things that would perhaps benefit the living when it is with the intention of doing others that benefit still more our posterity. And indeed, I would like it to be known that the little that I have learned up to now is almost nothing in comparison with what I do not know and do not despair of being able to learn. For it is almost the same with those who gradually discover truth in the [67] sciences as with those who, when they start to become rich, have less trouble making great acquisitions than they previously had when poor in making much lesser ones. Or they can be compared to captains of armies whose forces customarily grow in proportion to their victories, and who need more skill to maintain themselves after the loss of a battle than to capture villages and provinces after winning one. For truly it is giving battle when we try to conquer all the difficulties and errors that prevent us from attaining the knowledge of the truth, and it is to lose one when we accept some false opinion regarding a matter of some generality and importance. Afterwards, we need much more ability to regain the same state we were in than we need to make great progress when we already have assured principles. As for myself, if I have hitherto found some truths in the sciences (and I hope that the things contained in this volume will lead people to judge that I have found some), I can say that they only follow from and depend on five or six principal difficulties that I have overcome, and that I count as so many battles in which I have had luck on my side. I shall not even fear to say that I think I need to win only two or three more similar ones to accomplish completely the goal of my intentions, and that my age is not so advanced but that, in the ordinary course of nature, I may still have enough leisure for this result. [68] But I believe that I am so much the more obliged to take care of the time that remains to me as I have hope and power to use it well, and I would doubtless have many occasions to waste it if I were to publish the foundations of my physics. For while they are almost all so evident that it is only necessary to understand them to believe them, and there is none that I do not think I can demonstrate, nevertheless, because it is impossible that they should agree with all the diverse opinions of other men, I foresee that I would often be distracted by the opposition to which they would give birth.

It may be said that this opposition would be useful, both because it would make me recognize my mistakes and because, if I had something worthwhile, others might thereby have a better understanding of it and, as many can see further than one man alone, even now begin to use it and also help me with their discoveries. But although I recognize that I am extremely subject to error, and almost never trust the first thoughts that come to me, nevertheless the experience I have of the objections that can be made against me prevents me from hoping for any profit from them. For I have already often experienced the judgments of those I have considered as my friends as well as those of others to whom I thought myself indifferent, and also even of some whose malice and envy, I know, would work to discover what affection concealed from my friends. But it has rarely happened that something has been objected against me that I had not at all foreseen, unless it was [69] far removed from my subject, so that I have almost never encountered a critic of my opinions who did not seem to be either less rigorous or less equitable than myself. And I have never observed either that by means of the disputations that are practiced in the schools any truth has been discovered that was not known before. For while each tries to win, he exerts himself more in making the most of the probable than in weighing the arguments for one side and the other; and those who have been for a long time good lawyers are not afterwards, for that reason, better judges.

As for the utility that others would receive from the communication of my thoughts, it could not be very great, since I have not yet carried them so far that it would not be necessary to add many things before applying them to practice. And I think I can say without vanity that if there is someone who could do so, it must be me rather than someone else: not because there may not be many minds in the world incomparably better than mine, but because a thing cannot be so well conceived, and rendered one's own, when it is learned from someone else as when we have discovered it ourselves. This is so true in this matter that although I have often explained certain of my opinions to persons with very good minds, who, while I spoke to them, seemed to understand them very distinctly, nevertheless when they repeated them I noticed that they almost always changed them in such a way that I could no longer acknowledge them as mine. In this connection I would [70] like here to request those who will come after us never to believe that the things that will be said about my opinions come from me when I have not divulged them myself. And I am not at all astonished at the extravagances attributed to all those ancient philosophers whose writings we do not have, nor do I judge, for all that, that their thoughts were very unreasonable, since they were the best minds of their times, but only that they have been badly reported to us. For we also see that it almost never happens that any of their sectarians has surpassed them, and I am sure that the most impassioned of those who now follow Aristotle would believe themselves happy if they had as much knowledge of nature as he had, even on the condition that they would never have any more. They are like ivy, which does not try to climb higher than the trees that support it, and often even descends after it has reached the top.41 For it seems to me that those also descend, that is, make themselves somehow less learned than if they had abstained from study, who, not content with knowing all that is intelligibly explained in their author, try to find there in addition the solution of many difficulties of which he has said nothing and about which he has perhaps never thought. Nevertheless, their mode of philosophizing is most convenient for those who have only mediocre minds; for the obscurity of the distinctions and principles they use enables them to speak of all things as boldly as if they knew them, and to defend whatever they [71] say against the most subtle and capable, without there being any means of convincing them.

---

41 Lalande cites Bacon's *Great Instauration* as a possible source for this thought in "Some Texts of Bacon and Descartes," 66.

In this they seem to me like a blind man who, in order to fight without disadvantage against one who sees, makes him descend to the bottom of some extremely dark cave. And I may say that it is to their interest that I refrain from publishing the principles of the philosophy that I use; for they are so very simple and very evident that, if I were to publish them, it would be like opening some windows and bringing daylight into that cave where they have descended to fight. But even the best minds have no occasion to wish to know them; for if they wish to be able to speak about all things and to acquire the reputation of being learned, they will achieve this more easily by contenting themselves with probability, which can be found without great difficulty in all sorts of matters, than by searching for the truth, which is only discovered gradually in some of them, and which, when it is a question of speaking about other matters, obliges us to confess frankly that we do not know them. But if they prefer the knowledge of some few truths to the vanity of appearing ignorant of nothing, as doubtless it is quite preferable, and if they want to follow an intention similar to mine, they do not need for this goal that I tell them any more than I have already said in this discourse. For if they are capable of going beyond what I have done, they will also be all the more able to find by themselves all that I think I have found. And inasmuch as I have always examined everything in due order, it is certain that what still remains for me to discover is [72] in itself more difficult and concealed than what I have hitherto been able to encounter, and they would have much less pleasure in learning it from me than by themselves. Moreover, the habit that they will acquire of investigating easy things first, and passing by small degrees to more difficult ones, will serve them better than all my instruction could do. So, with regard to myself, I am persuaded that if I had been taught from my youth all the truths of which I have since sought the demonstrations, and had had no difficulty in learning them, I would perhaps have never known any others, and I would at least never have acquired the habit and the facility that I think I have of always finding new ones to the extent that I apply myself to seeking them. And in brief, if there is any work in the world that cannot be so well accomplished by anyone other than the one who has begun it, it is the one in which I am engaged.

It is true that one man alone cannot perform all the experiments that can be useful in it, but neither can he usefully employ other hands than his own, except for those of artisans or other such people that he could pay, and in whom the hope of gain, a most efficacious means, would move them to do with exactness everything he prescribed to them. For as for those volunteers who would perhaps offer to help him out of curiosity or desire to learn, aside from the fact that they usually promise more than they do, and only make beautiful proposals that never amount to anything, they [73] would infallibly want to be paid by the explanation of certain difficulties, or at least by useless compliments and conversations, which could not cost him so little time that he would not be the loser. And with regard to the experiments that others have already made, even if they were willing to communicate them to him, which those who call them secrets never would be, most of them consist of so many complications or superfluous ingredients that it would be very hard for him to decipher their truth. Besides, he would find almost all of them so badly explained or even so false, because those who have made them are forced to make them appear in agreement with their principles, that if there were some that were serviceable, they once again could not be worth the time that he would need to spend selecting them. Therefore if there were anyone in the world assuredly known to be capable of finding the things that are the greatest and most useful to the public that could be, so that other men were compelled to help him by every means to accomplish his intentions, I do not see that they could do anything for him but defray the expenses of the experiments he would need, and otherwise prevent his leisure from being taken up by anyone's importunity. But besides the fact that I do not presume so much of myself as to wish to promise anything extraordinary, nor to indulge in such vain thoughts as to imagine that the public should take great interest in my purposes, my soul is not so base that I would wish to accept from anyone [74] any favor that one might believe I had not merited.

All these considerations taken together were the cause that, three years ago, I did not want to divulge the treatise I had in hand, and that I had even resolved not to publish any other during my life that was so general, or by which the foundations of my physics could be understood. But since then there have been two other reasons that have obliged me to offer here certain particular essays, and to render to the public some account of my actions and my purposes. The first is that if I failed to do so, many who knew of my former intention to publish some writings could imagine that the reasons why I abstained were more to my disadvantage than they actually are. For although I do not love glory excessively, or even, if I dare say so, although I hate it insofar as I judge it contrary to the repose that I esteem higher than all else, nevertheless I have never tried to conceal my actions like crimes, nor have I ever taken great precautions to be unknown, both because I believed that I would be doing myself an injury, and because it would have caused me a kind of anxiety that once again would have been contrary to the perfect repose of mind that I seek. And because, having always remained indifferent to the concern with being known or not, I could not help acquiring some sort of reputation, I thought that I ought at least to do my best to keep from having a bad one. The other reason that obliged me to write [75] this is that I see more and more every day that my purpose to instruct myself suffers from the delay caused by the infinity of experiments that I require and that I cannot make without the help of others, and although I do not flatter myself so much as to expect that the public will be greatly concerned with my interests, nevertheless I also do not wish so to fail myself as to give those who will come after cause to reproach me some day because I could have left them many much better things if I had not been too negligent in letting them know how they could have contributed to my purposes.

And I thought that it would be easy for me to choose a few subjects that, without being subject to too much controversy, or obliging me to declare more of my principles than I desire, would not fail to show with sufficient clarity what I can or cannot do in the sciences. I cannot say whether I have succeeded in this, and I do not want to influence anyone's judgment by speaking about my writings. But I will be glad to have them examined, and in order for there to be so much the more occasion to do so, I beg all those who have some objections to make to take the pains to send them to my publisher, and after I am informed of them I will try to join my reply to them at the same time; and by this means readers who see them both together can judge more easily of the truth. For I do not promise ever to make long replies to them but only to admit my errors very frankly, if I perceive them, or [76] if I do not, to say simply what I believe to be required for the defense of the things I have written, without adding the explanation of any new matter, in order not to be endlessly involved in one thing after another.

But if some of the things I have said at the beginning of the *Dioptrics* and the *Meteors* are at first shocking because I call them suppositions and seem to have no desire to prove them, the reader should have the patience to read the whole attentively, and I trust he will find himself satisfied. For it seems to me that the reasons are interconnected in such a way that, just as the last ones are demonstrated by the first, which are their causes, so the first are reciprocally proved by the last, which are their effects. And it must not be imagined that in this I commit the error that logicians call reasoning in a circle. For since experience renders most of these effects very certain, the causes from which I deduce them serve not so much to prove them as to explain them; on the contrary, it is the causes that are proved by the effects. And I have called them suppositions only so that it may be known that I think they can be deduced from those first truths that I have explained above, but I have wished deliberately not to do so, to prevent certain minds, who imagine that they know in one day all that another has thought in twenty years as soon as he has told them but two or three words, and who are the more subject to error and less capable of the truth as they are more penetrating and quick, from [77] taking the opportunity to build on what they believe to be my principles some extravagant philosophy for which I would be blamed. For as for the opinions that are wholly mine, I do not defend them as being new, since if the reasons for them are considered carefully, I am sure that they will be found to be so simple and so conformable to common sense that they will seem less extraordinary and less strange than any others that one might have on the same subjects. And I also do not boast of being the first discoverer of any of them, but rather that I have accepted them neither because they have been asserted by others nor because they have not been, but only because reason has persuaded me of them.

If artisans cannot immediately carry out the invention that is explained in the *Dioptrics*, I do not believe that it should therefore be said that it is bad; for since it requires skill and practice to make and adjust the machines that I have described so that no detail is missing, I would be no less astonished if they succeeded on the first attempt than if someone were able to learn to play the lute excellently in one day by merely being given a good fingering chart. And if I write in French, which is the language of my country, rather than in Latin, which is that of my preceptors, it is because I hope that those who use only their natural reason in its purity will judge better of my opinions than those who believe only in ancient books. As for those who join good sense with study, who are the only judges I desire, [78] they will not be, I am sure, so partial to Latin that they refuse to listen to my reasonings because I explain them in the vernacular.

For the rest, I do not wish to speak here in detail of the progress I hope to make in the sciences in the future, or to bind myself to the public with any promise that I am not confident of fulfilling. I will only say that I have resolved to employ the rest of my life only in trying to acquire some knowledge of nature from which can be derived rules for medicine more assured than those we have had up to the present, and that my inclination is so far removed from other purposes, especially those that can be useful to some only by being harmful to others, that if circumstances compelled me to adopt them, I do not believe that I would be capable of succeeding. Regarding this I make a declaration here that I well know cannot help to make me important in the world, but then I have no desire to be so; and I will always hold myself more obliged to those by whose favor I enjoy without hindrance my leisure than to those who offer me the most honorable positions on earth.

Interpretive Essay:
Descartes's *Discourse on Method*

The *Discourse on Method* is a very famous book, but it is also quite unsatisfactory. It is, of course, not a book in one sense but an introduction to a volume that contains, in addition, three other writings—three scientific writings—the *Dioptrics*, the *Geometry*, and the *Meteors*. Now why is this book so widely read, as widely read perhaps as any philosophical book? Its appeal seems to be, first, that it is autobiography. It is rare for a philosopher presumably concerned with the universal, the timeless, to spend so much time telling us the particular details of his own life. Autobiographies are written by statesmen or by movie actresses or shall we say by retired surgeons, but very rarely by philosophers, that is, until modern philosophy—that is, beginning with Descartes. After Descartes we have of course Vico; we have something that looks like autobiography, called the *Confessions* of Rousseau. Descartes seems to establish a genre. Now we catch on to the trick of Descartes's book fairly quickly. The stages of his life are not only correlated with, but in fact identical with, parts of his philosophic system. This means that we acquire the whole of Descartes's philosophy in an effortless but very unsatisfactory way. Nothing in this book is really thought through or at least carefully and adequately reasoned through. And so we are left to wonder what Descartes had in mind when he wrote the system as the story of his life.

A glance at the table of contents tells us where to look to answer this question. In the sixth and last part, Descartes says that the author will supply the reasons that caused him to write; and so as a kind of timesaver, I shall turn directly to the last part of the *Discourse*. It begins very quietly and soberly. He was about to publish a treatise when he heard that a certain opinion in physics had been condemned by an authority, and he grants that authority a certain place. He does not name the person that was condemned or the book that was condemned or the authorities that condemned them. The reticence is hollow because everyone at that time would know that the author of that book was Galileo, that the condemned doctrine was Copernicanism, and that the authority that condemned it was the Holy Office, more often referred to as the Inquisition. He doesn't have to spell that out because his readers already know it. He says that this book, so far as he could tell prior to the condemnation, as far as his reason could tell him, was not harmful to church or to state. Reason, that is, is no guide to what you can publish. So he suppressed the book. That's my first point: we must note the theological-political situation after the condemnation of Galileo. This is the "hermeneutic situation" of the *Discourse on Method.*

The condemnation of opinions advanced by philosophers is nothing new. The new thing follows, and this is my second point. Descartes does not in fact really say that he wishes to argue that there ought to be freedom of speech or that Galileo should be allowed to publish that book. He does not offer the kind of argument for the freedom of publication that we in the twentieth century somehow automatically read in. No, the new thing is that the situation is intolerable for a second and different reason that now enters the scene. The new thing Descartes has discovered on the basis of his physics, rather by chance—we have to keep our eye on that—is this: suddenly after completing his philosophy, but especially his physics, he discovers the possibility that philosophy no longer needs to be theoretical, which means no longer concerned with knowledge of first principles of the whole sought for their own sake. That whole tradition of "speculative philosophy" may now be laid aside in favor of "practical philosophy." And it is here that he introduces that memorable praise of practical philosophy: it will make us humans the "masters and owners of nature." He now argues in detail why this will be of immense potential benefit to all mankind, in three fundamental ways. It will produce, first of all, an infinity of inventions that will satisfy our physical needs; second, it will produce a genuinely scientific medicine, a medicine that will produce health, "the first good and the foundation of all other goods of this life"; third, it will lead to a kind of new practical wisdom, based somehow on this peculiar science, medicine—peculiar, because the medicine is not what we normally think of as medicine but a science of the acute dependence of the mind on the body.

Now, the third reason why Descartes publishes arises from the first two. Since the public or humanity is to benefit from this project, Descartes turns to the public to support his project, which means not only the public but also the rulers of the public. They must support the project, and thereby alter the theological-political situation after Galileo. Now we understand immediately from that why the first fact of the *Discourse*—its popular style—is absolutely crucial. But of course it is not the public but young philosophers and scientists who will carry out and complete Descartes's work. And no matter how popular the writing is, Descartes is emphatic that he has placed in the book quite enough for intelligent readers to take their bearings by and to carry on his endeavor—he means in the *Discourse* together with the three scientific treatises that accompany it. Since the book must persuade the public and their rulers to alter the theological-political situation, but is also addressed to philosophers and scientists, it is necessarily written on two planes. And we shall find abundant evidence of that. You could say that rhetorically the book has this double addressee, public and philosopher. If you think about it, it also has two opponents: first, the Church, which is sedulously distinguished from the secular political authorities in the context—the Church insofar as it is an obstacle to this project; and second, theoretical or speculative philosophy—mainly Aristotelianism. But one can combine those, of course: the name by which we join together those two great powers is "Scholasticism" or *L'Ecole*.

With these first intimations of Descartes's intentions in the *Discourse*, we are ready to start at the beginning. The first thesis in Part 1 is that good sense or reason is by nature equal in all men. Later on he will flatly contradict this. In Part 2 and at a still later point he will argue that some men are naturally much stupider than others; for example, even the most stupid man can invent sign language. That is, the first thesis in the *Discourse* is an example of the use of deliberate contradiction. What is the point of this contradiction? We begin with the first thought, so familiar to us. Our good sense or reason is equal because everybody is satisfied with as much as he's got. Notice that the beginning is quite pleasing: you don't have to envy anybody. But of course, it's also a fallacy. It's an old French proverb that Descartes picked up in Montaigne. If you notice that it's a fallacy, of course, you're especially pleased, but this time with your own superiority. Everybody's pleased! It's a very pleasant beginning. This is irony, in the most technical sense of the word, addressing two different thoughts to two kinds of readers in one and the same sentence. Descartes in the first sentence of the first paragraph gives us a little ABC "how to read me" lesson.

But it actually goes on for five paragraphs, which you could call the proem to the book. It has an interesting movement—something like this: Paragraph 1: All men are by nature equal. Paragraph 2: I, however, am inferior to other men in certain perfections of mind, imagination, memory, and so on. Paragraph 3: I was lucky; I happened to find a method that made me a philosopher and superior to other men. Paragraph 4: Maybe, however, I'm fooling myself—like a deluded alchemist who thought he discovered the philosophers' stone. Therefore

I will level with you and simply tell you the story of my life. Paragraph 5: The story of my life, however, is a history, or if you prefer, a fable. Everybody, I hope, will thank me for my frankness, on the old principle that everybody thinks an author means exactly what he understands in the author. But that Descartes intends the duality of level, of the *Discourse* as history and fable, becomes perfectly clear because shortly afterwards the terms "history" and "fable" come back in again. Generally speaking, fables simulate and histories dissimulate, and histories must be "read with discretion"—that is Descartes's recipe for reading the *Discourse*. Putting this together we ask: have we learned anything about the autobiographical character or the work? Yes. Autobiographic form is a device that dissimulates superiority. Descartes is able to speak on the plane of autobiography while at the same time indicating via that same autobiography a different level of teaching. This means that we often have to interpret this book on the public level before we find its arguments. We'll come back to that in just a moment.

The argument proper of the *Discourse* begins in the heart of Part 1 with Descartes's critique of his college education. He starts with a goal: clear and assured knowledge useful for life. He claims that he was taught that goal by his Jesuit teachers. At the end of this college discussion, he reiterates that goal, only this time he calls it not clear and assured knowledge useful for life but useful for *this* life. He has left his Jesuit instructors behind in one decisive respect. This principle, call it certainty for the sake of utility, in this life, is the first principle of Descartes's methodology. In reading this book, we have to distinguish between the method—the four rules that we find in Part 2—and the methodology, the more general guiding principles out of which comes the method proper. The whole book is *Discourse on Method*, that is, *logos* on method, that is, methodology. The word is a nineteenth-century word but the thought is Descartes's. The methodology will come down to a small number of guiding principles. In the particulars of his education only one thing, mathematics, is certain and nothing is really useful, useful for life. Certainty is one thing, utility another. Do the two ever come together? Now, initially, Descartes surely leaves the impression that he seeks certain knowledge of the useful; thus, in that way, the two would be united. That would mean, for example, mathematical knowledge—knowledge as certain as mathematics—of the goals of human life. This he never attains, and, if we observe carefully, never really attempts. It is not really his notion that we can apply a doctrine of certainty in any of its forms, mathematical or methodical, to the question of the good.

The quest for certainty is much more obtrusive in the book. It is spelled out through a series of steps: mathematical method, metaphysics (which is said to be even more certain than mathematics), and mathematical physics. It surely supplies premises or conditions for the other inquiry, which is about utility, as articulated into the knowledge of the goals of life or the goods of life. While certainty is always in the foreground, the other inquiry, into the good life, is ultimately distinct. It is always based on experience, and it is never certain. That is, the more fundamental, that which supplies the direction, is always on the plane of the empirical. The certainty-utility distinction is the ancestor of the distinction familiar to us between facts and values, but this ancestry can be misleading, since Descartes never restricts knowledge to the certain. The ultimate guiding knowledge is always of the goal, the end, the useful, and it is never certain. The primary question is "what is the right life?" and in that respect Descartes is clearly in the Socratic tradition. In the *Discourse*, these themes are developed in alternation: the certainty of method in Part 2; Part 3, morality, which is uncertain; Parts 4 and 5, metaphysics and physics, which belong in the sphere of certainty; and finally, utility—that means the end, that means the uncertain again—returns in Part 6.

The sphere of certainty is a program that has to be developed. But the utility or the good has to be discussed immediately. Otherwise Descartes does not know where he is going. But where is this initial reflection on the useful or good? The answer is conveyed through the particulars of his autobiography plus certain general remarks, for example, about ancient morals. He gives us the basis for this principle of interpretation by the following argument: He was studying in one of the best schools in Europe. Europe in his century was as flourishing and fertile in great minds as in any previous time. He was judged by others to be the equal of his fellow students and thought so himself, and the students were destined to replace the masters. That means that he is the equal of any man that ever lived in the tradition, in philosophy, theology, liberal arts, and so on. He has elevated himself by the argument to the position where he can claim that his particular judgment is worthy of consideration as a general verdict upon the tradition of arts and letters, which means the whole tradition of learning including philosophy and theology. Every particular biographical detail, then, has potential general meaning, and we have to enucleate this general meaning often out of particular facts.

In Part 1, the reflection on the good leads to this general view, if we put together some of these details: Our reason, human reason, is exclusively in the service of our own interests or subordinate to the passions or the desires. And the desires do not include a particular desire to know, to know for its own sake. I call this the natural egoism of reason. Initially, as you recall from the very first paragraph, the stress is on how egoism distorts our reason: good sense is equal because each man is satisfied with as much as he has, because each man's ego thinks as well as possible of itself. Ego distorts reason. But at the end of Part 1, after Descartes's travels, he says that he has learned—and this is obviously an empirical inference—that "the reason of each" (the phrase is identical in the first paragraph) is sound when it is concerned with what is immediately before one on those occasions when an error causes pain. And it is sounder than the speculations of the men of letters. That is, it is sounder than those who are concerned, so they think or so they say, with knowledge for its own sake. That supposed concern is simply an attempt to be superior to "common sense"; it is vanity. We know from the later passage about "speculation," and its rejection for the sake of mastery of nature, that it is one of Descartes's key terms. The rejection of speculation or of speculative philosophy here is really on the plane of a general thesis about all men's nature. This primary level of critique is on the plane of the human soul as such. Hence in the whole *Discourse* Descartes never says that there is a natural desire for knowledge, or that philosophy begins in wonder. In the decisive context for this issue (*Discourse* 5, near the end), when he asks "what is man?" he first compares man to machines and then says that the same principles that distinguish man and machines apply equally to the difference between man and animals. It is in that context, where he says what man is, that he says what reason is. Reason is necessary and it is described as an instrument—a universal instrument, but an instrument. That is the conclusion already prepared by the natural egoism of reason. Since reason serves the passions, and doesn't naturally seek knowledge, it needs to be conducted. Hence the title of the book, *Discourse on the Method for Conducting the Reason Well*. Descartes goes on to add: *and Seeking for Truth in the Sciences*. The title's duality mirrors the utility-certainty duality that we were speaking of before. Thus, for Descartes it is the nature of the soul, which demands that reason be conducted, that leads up to the method proper.

How does Descartes establish this proposition? If you deny natural egoism, then you talk about virtue as did the ancient writings on morals, lofty and splendid but built on sand, or without any real knowledge of how you acquire it. What is needed is the low and solid foundation for morality or virtue, namely, the foundation of natural egoism. Consider a second example. If you do pursue knowledge for its own sake, as had been claimed by the whole philosophic tradition, what is the result? Endless disputes without resolution, and nothing so strange or incredible that it hasn't been maintained by some philosopher. And if the philosophers had found the truth or if they had been honestly in quest of it for its own sake, would they not have found it? This last argument is, of course, troublesome because it suggests that the truth must be essentially simple. If men had found it, they would have been able to convince each other and put an end to the dispute. But can the truth about the first principles of all things, of the whole, be essentially simple? There is another possibility, namely, that the truth which the philosophers sought, the truth of ultimate principles, is either unavailable or is unnecessary or both. The first principles may be replaced by methodology, and that is, in fact, what I shall be advancing as a reading of this book.

By the end of Part 1, Descartes has advanced the notion that all men naturally pursue their own good, although some men naturally have more reason than others. So Descartes asks, "What way of life should I follow? What is the good for me?"—for a naturally superior man. Part 2 develops this question of the good, and then Descartes tries to make the certainty and the need for method emerge out of the good. Since philosophy, traditionally understood, is evidently not the good life, whereas other human pursuits evidently are useful, Descartes asks the question in what the perfection of these pursuits consists. It is a meditation on perfection. Perfection is more probable if the activity is conceived and executed by one master. That is especially true in the arts: and the arts are recognizably useful and benevolent human activities. Furthermore, all human activities, if well carried out, have the character of art. In addition, the arts have a structure; they in certain cases include others or are more comprehensive than others. The builder of the house comes under the one who plans the city, and he, in turn, under the legislator who lays down laws for a whole people or nation. Since the arts as such are benevolent, the most comprehensive is the most benevolent, always assuming, of course, that it was the work of one and not of many. Finally, Descartes takes the step that reasoning itself, or philosophy, may be considered as an art. That means that philosophy is considered as a form of mastery. But it must be made one, or it must be purified of its manyness. Descartes traces its manyness both to the variety of teachers that we have and to the fact that owing to our nature, reason develops much later than our passions and our senses. That disproportion in human nature has to be overcome; mastery of human nature is the first condition of mastery of nature simply. Several purgations of both kinds of manyness are necessary, and that points directly to the model of that which owes nothing to nature, to the senses, or to teachers, namely, the truths of geometry and mathematics.

This project—a word Descartes uses in this context—could be just a vain hope. Most of the arguments that we've been using about mastery and about perfection through mastery are taken without acknowledgment from Francis Bacon's book on method, the *New Organon*, published seventeen years before. In that book, there was a long section, thirteen aphorisms, on reasons why the human race can have hope, ultimately thanks to a methodical science of nature. But Descartes doesn't need to argue that we need to have hope: he already had a science of nature before he dreamed of "mastery." While he is proceeding in a series of arguments here in *Discourse*, Part 2—from the argument about mastery to the need for purification of reason to the need for method—his own life proceeded in the opposite sequence. Before he ever imagined that philosophy could be understood as mastery, he had fully conceived and executed a universal method and shown that this could be successfully applied to the science of the physical world. In an earlier fragment called the *Regulae* there is not a whisper of an argument about mastery, but there is a fully developed argument about mathematical method. This earlier fragment is plainly not a quest for first principles, and therefore the question arises, what is the intention of philosophy? In that book there is hardly any answer. Between the *Regulae* and the *Discourse* Descartes learned from Francis Bacon that the end, since it cannot be theoretical, must be understood practically. That means that the book we are reading is, in its apparent biographical sequence, in fact the reverse of the truth, or it is a fable, not history.

One could say that that's not quite sufficient—that it is still the story of this unique man, suitably modified, that tells us that it is his unique passion for mastery, his unique natural temperament, his ego, which explains why it is a model. In other words, by gathering the inner truth of the autobiographical account, we don't leave the ego of Descartes behind. No, we simply understand its thought in the correct philosophical sequence by retaining the crucial importance of the fact that his whole project had to be conceived in one ego of a certain kind, namely, that of Descartes. As regards that egoism, we have the notions of mastery and perfection and of benevolence. We do not yet have the notion of the recognition for the benevolence, or glory, except for a statement in Part 1 where Descartes says, "I do not despise glory as do the Cynics." That's a clue to his willingness to acknowledge glory as part of the good. To summarize this point, we move from the natural egoism that is common to all men to the peculiar egoism of this man, his quest for mastery, and both of the stages will be prior to and conditions for the epistemological ego that will emerge in the famous sentence from Part 4, "I think, therefore I am."

At this point, in between mastery and method, there is a political interlude, a kind of acknowledgment that Descartes is on a collision course with society. He must purge his reason; he must doubt all belief and opinion. But what are belief and opinion? They are the bond, the constitutive bond, of these "great bodies," as he calls them, societies. Therefore, his reform must be kept absolutely private. If he were to publish the necessity for doubting all belief, he could be reasonably accused, he says, of attempting a new reformation, a word he uses twice in the context. Remember the year: 1637. What's going on at that time? The Thirty Years' War, that is, the war whose primary, though not sole, cause is the Reformation. This whole part of the *Discourse*, Parts 2 and 3, begins with allusions to the war that's going on. We must connect "reformation" with those particular wars. Since he says, "I am only going to reform my own thoughts," it might seem that Descartes is politically a conformist, an upholder of the status quo. That would be plausible if he didn't publish the fact that he is obliged to doubt all his beliefs. Moreover, the conclusion would be acceptable if Descartes didn't discuss at some length the problem of reforming these great bodies and indicate that reformation is primarily a matter not of legitimacy but of prudence, that is, of success. Descartes, furthermore, leaves no doubt that the extant political states are all in need of reform. At this point Descartes doesn't have any new political doctrine. But we know in reading this part that we are reading a published book. So this private man did eventually publish his demand for the doubt of all opinions, and thereby indicate that he has in mind some sort of reformation. Reform will require disciples, imitators. The world is almost totally made up two kinds of men who ought not to imitate his model. The first kind is too hasty and impetuous; the second are those who have enough reason, or enough modesty, to know they don't have enough reason to imitate Descartes. You can see he wants a man who is persevering, who avoids precipitancy in employing the method, who has superior brains, and is immodest. In that way, while telling you that "almost" the whole world is made up of those two kinds who should not imitate him, he has of course exactly specified the kind of men that should imitate him. I think that's one of the clearest places in the entire work where you see a distinction of kinds of readers of Descartes. The peculiar kind of reformation has already been indicated: change the theological-political situation so that the project of mastery of nature can begin to develop and benefit mankind.

In approaching the method proper, we are at a great disadvantage, because we have presented here in words a method that is in principle mathematical. Descartes, I think, intends us to read this section in light of the whole argument, the method in the light, shall we say, of the methodology. For example, immediately following the four rules of method, Descartes makes a general proposal: all the things that fall within the knowledge of man, he imagines, could be interconnected by deductive chains of reasoning, just as we find in geometry. He imagines, that is, a kind of universal deductive system of everything. And yet that has to be corrected by what we have already seen and shall see: the applicability of method is partial. Neither the reflections on the good that have preceded nor those that follow can be mathematicized, nor can they be studied by the four rules of method. To anticipate, we cannot demonstrate mathematically, and we do not need to demonstrate, the fundamental premises, that pain is bad and pleasure is good. You can deny those truths without contradicting yourself, but they are as certain for any living human being as any principle of mathematics.

We shall say a few things about the rules of method just to indicate what is involved without really explaining them adequately. The rules of the method are meant to point to a set of algebraic operations. Descartes's algebra uses algebraic symbols, that is, algebraic signs, not only as symbols of arithmetic qualities (numerical amounts), but also as symbols of geometric magnitude. But, in addition, geometric figures can in turn symbolize both algebraic symbols and arithmetic amounts. That is bewildering. Thinking it through, what is at work is that the intrinsic intelligible differences between the kind of entities that you're studying in arithmetic, say numbers, and the kind of entities you're studying in geometry, that is, lines, and so on, or the distinction between discrete quantity and continuous quantity—all those differences can be ignored by the right technique. We know that, after Descartes, it came to be called analytic geometry. Now what else can we say about this method? The third rule says that we devise an order of inquiry—we invent one—if a natural order of inquiry is not available. That is, method to be certain need not be guided by any natural articulation that we ordinarily find in things. All that's necessary is that you have the certainty of the starting point, which makes possible a deductive sequence from that point forward. Essentially, the tactic is to find in the analysis of the terms of any problem the starting point, the simples, as he calls them, which are irreducible to anything else and which may be combined and brought into relation, and stated in algebraic symbols, and so on. If you think about it, what Descartes is advocating is that you do not start from where we naturally stand, that is to say, as human beings who have sense perception and opinions, and from that point seek to understand the phenomena and somehow to get access to more fundamental principles. This characteristic starting point, which one could say with some reason is the natural starting point of philosophy, is abolished by this methodological procedure. Another way of putting it would be that Descartes's intent is to find a starting point not in the prearticulated kinds of beings, but rather in principles that cut across the natural articulations. What sort of things would they be? Laws! Mathematical laws that govern all kinds of bodies, whether they be animals, plants, or whatever. Now there is a silence, a darkness in the argument here. What is it that Descartes is claiming to know? Only at a somewhat later point do we see that nature is understood by him as body, and as extended body. Now finally, and in a way most crucial, the simple thing about method is that method is not only a way of discovering but also a guarantee of knowledge. We usually distinguish between discovery and validity in recent discussions of methodology, but that distinction is not at all acknowledged by Descartes. Method of discovery is identical with method of validation, or verification, if you like. That means if you learn something by the method, it deserves, owing to the methodological procedure, to be called "knowledge." There is no necessity that you trace the causes of what you know to still more general or higher causes. At each step, in short, you have a fully guaranteed claim to know, thanks to the methodological procedure. For example, we don't need to understand bodies in terms of the ultimate parts or particles. This demand for ultimacy is one meaning of the traditional term "metaphysics," and we shall have to keep our eye on this matter because our initial judgment, reading the discussion of method proper, is that there is no need for metaphysics—no need for a further warrant, no need for a quest for the causes or ultimate principles underlying these causes. But that seems to be contradicted later in the *Discourse*. Since this contradiction makes the metaphysical discussion in Part 4 of great importance, I am going to some extent to slight the contribution of Part 3, the provisional morality.

Descartes says elsewhere that he put this morality in the book in order to persuade pedagogues that he was not against religion. When we read it, its piety isn't all that persuasive. For example, rule one says "Conform": conform to the laws, customs, and religion of my country— that means the laws, customs, and religion of Catholic France—or, he says, to the most moderate opinions wherever you are. But you may be in Persia or in China—you see how loyal he is to the laws, customs, and Roman Catholicism of France, or to the Christianity of Europe. But, he goes on, "conform to what people do, rather than to what they say, because in the corruption of our morals, there are few people who want to say all they believe." That belongs again to our rhetorical problem: why the double level of speech? Well, here's one reason: because of the corruption of morals, few people "want to say" all they believe. In Part 6 he says, "I do not *want to say* that I agree with Galileo." He indicates quite clearly in that way, by this very precise repetition of the phrase, that he did agree with Galileo. Now, "conform" apparently means even to despotism or tyranny, so long as it leaves you alone to philosophize. But some countries are better than others, and at the end of Part 3 he goes to live in a country, Holland, where they leave you alone, at least more than elsewhere.

Rule two says "Be resolute," persevere in one direction. The four rules have a kind of rhythm: rule one, externally, conform; rule two, internally, be resolute; rule three, externally, conform, this time not to society, but rather to the order of the world; rule four, internally, find your satisfaction and contentment in the continued pursuit of the truth. None of these four rules is clear and distinct in the strict sense of the method. "Clear and distinct" in the strict sense means what cannot be doubted. And the indubitable is that whose denial produces a contradiction. None of these moral principles has that character. Therefore the statement in the table of contents that he drew his morality from his method cannot mean that he drew his moral rules from the rules of the method. What it means is that the necessity for a provisional morality, and certain fundamental characteristics of that morality, are created by the adoption of the method. For example, because you do not take your bearings by the natural articulation of things, as is implied in the method, you are in the situation as described in rule two, you are in a forest—you do not know where you are. That is to say, the world around you does not supply any articulation; therefore, you adopt a direction and persevere, regardless of what seems to be around you or how the world seems to be articulated.

Rule three is particularly interesting, because it is about mastery. It seems to be just the opposite of what we've been construing Descartes to say in Part 2. The rule begins by saying, "I agree with the Stoics, don't try to master fortune or change the order of the world, but only master your own thoughts." When we follow this through, we see that Descartes is not really a Stoic. He is a satirist of the Stoics. For example, he says if you should follow this splendid precept, you would not want to be healthy if you are sick—after all, only your thoughts are in your power and you don't concern yourself with what's outside your thoughts. You will not want to be healthy if you are sick, or be free if you are in jail, any more than you want to fly like the birds or have a body as incorruptible as diamonds. In this absurd manner, in short, the Stoics thought they could rival the gods, but only by forgetting their humanity, their corporeality, and their mortality. The limits of what is in human power now are not identical with what can ever come within human power. We have to correct for this satirical element in order to make the third moral rule agree with the mastery arguments that preceded it and with the great stress on health and medicine that will follow. The fourth moral rule is not really a moral rule, but states the goal that underlies the other three rules, namely, to continue to pursue the truth. Here we find two very innocent words, contentment and satisfaction. They recur in a technical sense in many contexts in Descartes. Contentment means a state that reflects the general character, the goodness of one entire life that has been chosen. Satisfaction is the pleasure that attends a particular activity, here the discovery of the truth. Both belong together as kind of a refined hedonism that has as yet no moral relation to other human beings, except the negative one that we have seen in rule one, conformism. Descartes is silent here about what it is that he knows that is so pleasant. But already by the end of Part 3 it seems quite clear that he has embarked upon some of the fundamental researches of his physics and he alludes to some of the inquiries embodied in the accompanying three treatises. Nonetheless, he argues in the sequel that the science of physics must not, as that would suggest, precede metaphysics; it could not, for it must derive from metaphysics. So we must consider the metaphysics, and then see the relation to physics.

In Part 4, Descartes treats three of the traditional problems of metaphysics. The first is substance, what it means to be, in any and every case in which we say something is. The second is the question of the ultimate, what is first, the cause or principle of the whole. The third traditional problem is truth. Descartes says that the human soul is a substance, that God is the first or ultimate thing, and that truth is clarity and distinctness. That appears to be fairly traditional metaphysics, vaguely Aristotelian. Looked at more precisely, it supports Christian doctrine and so is traditional in a second sense. The human soul is an independent substance that can exist apart from body; God in an omnipotent being; and clear and distinct ideas are true ideas only if they are guaranteed by God. That is, all three doctrines, taken in a more precise sense, offer considerable support to orthodox religious apologetics. Indeed, you can say, the implications of these metaphysical doctrines appear to offer a more direct support to Christian apologetics than the arguments that we find in Thomas Aquinas. They face two ways: toward foundations of philosophy, but also toward rational corroboration of Christian faith.

Consider the first argument, about the soul. Descartes says that after having doubted many things, including especially body, he cannot doubt that he exists, and since doubting is thinking, "I think, therefore I am" is true. This principle—the *cogito* as we call it for short—is "the first principle of my philosophy." It is the first principle not because it is the most certain: obviously it presupposes the principle of noncontradiction.

It is first because it enables Descartes to solve a problem, the relation of mind to the world. There is a double requirement: the knowing or thinking of mind must be pure of influences on the mind, without the being of mind being hopelessly separated from the world. How does this happen? The knowledge that he is a thinking thing does not depend on knowledge that he is a bodily being. Thus, the thinking of the thinking thing is epistemologically independent of the world of bodies—that guarantees the epistemological independence of mind from the world. But it is not independent in being—not metaphysically independent. The fact that I know only that I am a thinking thing does not mean that I am only a thinking thing, that is, a mind whose existence is independent of the existence of body. Yet Descartes does draw this conclusion: mind or soul is a separate substance, independent of body, and therefore could be immortal. That supports religious apologetics. But Descartes waffles: he admits that the argument for an independent soul is fallacious in the preface to the *Meditations*. So we must separate the solid conclusion— epistemological independence—from the fallacious conclusion— metaphysical independence—that supports the apologetics. The solid argument does not imply that mind or soul is a substance: we have to separate the solid from the metaphysical.

Consider now point two, the existence of God. Descartes argues from an idea in the mind in both of his proofs of the existence of God. That is, he does not argue, as Thomas Aquinas had argued, from nature to God. There is no ascent from nature to God because Cartesian nature shows no evidence of being made by God. Cartesian nature is mechanism. "The laws of nature," says Descartes, "are the same as the laws of mechanics." Since mechanism is devoid of purposes, nature shows no evidence of the purposes of God. Thus Cartesian physics, in its mechanistic character, determines in this negative way the character of the proofs for God's existence: they cannot begin with nature. The sequence of the *Discourse*, first metaphysics, then physics, is the reverse of the true sequence. But if nature shows no evidence of a divine author, then this theocentric metaphysics is in profound discord with the Bible. That discord is kept out of sight in Part 4, because theocentric metaphysics is positioned before physics puts in an appearance in Part 5.

Consider now the third point, truth. Descartes argues that truth is clarity and distinctness. First, he proves that God exists, using clear and distinct ideas; then he says that God is the guarantor of clear and distinct ideas. That is the Cartesian circle, a famous problem. But it is, of course, strong support for religious apologetics: all our ideas, including especially truth, depend on God. If you think about the argument, it is a very interesting interpretation of omnipotence. If an omnipotent

God exists, then it follows that he was the cause of your thinking at each step of the prior argument, just as he is the cause of everything. Circularity of argument, in short, is unavoidable: if God is omnipotent, then circularity of human reasoning is unavoidable, and philosophy becomes problematic.

Did Descartes wish to undermine philosophy in order to support a religious apologetics? Precisely the theocentric character of the metaphysics undermines the rationality of philosophy while seeming to support apologetics. But now we observe something new: the apologetics itself is designed only to persuade a relatively low human type, what Descartes calls "weak minds" (*esprits faibles*). "Next to the denial of God, nothing leads weak minds away from virtue more than the denial of the immortality of the soul," he asserts in the last paragraph of Part 5. Descartes is not a weak mind, but a man of good sense, an *esprit fort*, a strong mind. Since Descartes does not himself need apologetics— neither he nor his disciples—we wonder whether he needs theocentric metaphysics. It now appears that he prefers philosophy to the theocentric metaphysics that jeopardizes philosophy. The metaphysics proves to be divorcible from his philosophy. This divorce first appears in the divorce of physics from metaphysics.

From Part 4, we have learned that there is no ascent from things or nature to God as their author or first cause. Is there not, however, a descent from God to nature? If there is neither ascent nor descent, to or from God, then God has no relation at all to nature. God would be redundant in the Cartesian philosophy. Descartes must descend from God to nature, or descend from God as the author of nature to nature, if he wishes to preserve a harmony between his philosophy and the Bible. The laws of nature must be shown to be compatible with the biblical account of creation—that's the first problem of Part 5. It is obviously not fundamental for the question of Copernicanism in Galileo, who did not even know the laws of nature in this sense. As regards the action of God, we have to be quite careful and enumerate precisely what is attributed to him. God has established laws of nature and has imprinted ideas of these laws on our souls. Moreover, God has created matter sufficient to form the world. And he agitated the matter in diverse ways so that it obeys the laws of nature. He does nothing else. That is, in the beginning, God created chaos, but a chaos of bodies that obeyed the laws of nature, out of which, bit by bit, slowly over eons of time, evolved the physical world as we know it, the sun, the solar system, the earth, and on the earth, plants. Animals—that's a problem: Descartes cannot deduce them. In the sequel, he has to make two corrections in this account. The ideas of laws of nature are imprinted in us. They are innate. But the ideas of those laws in us do not tell us that God is the author of those laws. So Descartes has to correct the account. The reasons for the laws of nature are derived from the infinite perfections of God, he says. This gives us a link, a kind of cognitive descent, from God to the laws. But it does not tell us that God established the laws. Creation is still moot, of course. Moreover, we can ask from which perfections of God does Descartes derive these laws. No answer is forthcoming here in the *Discourse*. Surely not from his omnipotence or omniscience, for this God of Descartes is allowed to do very little. He does as little as possible, and lets the laws and the evolution of time do almost everything. He is remarkably underemployed, if he possesses all of these infinite attributes. But, of course, we have the other book, *The World*, which is being summarized in *Discourse* 5. There Descartes does use one of the divine attributes—immutability—and says that from immutability he deduced the laws of nature. This means that the laws of nature are immutable, but it does not tell you what they are and what their content is. So Descartes is reduced to saying—this is, in a way, the conclusion—that God preserves the laws. His preservation of the laws is equivalent to the action by which he at first created the world. This is an old doctrine, advanced by certain medieval theologians, to reconcile divine creation with the eternity of the universe. Descartes uses it in *Discourse* 5 and the effect is that since God now only preserves the world in being—and that is the meaning of creation—God has not established anything. The world is now the same as it has ever been, coexistent with God. That is the second correction. Since neither the character of the laws nor the things that emerge thanks to them show evidence of being made by a benevolent deity, the descent from God to nature is at best empty. Neither by ascent nor by descent is God related to Cartesian nature.

We now, I think, approach the deeper level of Cartesian philosophy. We have been pursuing one metaphysical issue, the question of ultimacy or first ultimate principles. We have seen that the relation of God to nature is simulated or empty, and that tells us that the relation of the Bible and creation, on the one hand, and the new physics, on the other, is negative or one of mutual exclusiveness. This simulation only hides from us the deeper problem, that there is no ultimate principle whatever. The phrase "laws of nature" seems to imply a divine lawgiver. But none is in fact necessary. That is to say, there's no reason in principle why we can't move directly from method to laws of nature. And that Descartes does in earlier books. The simulation of the divine lawgiver serves to dissimulate the absence of any metaphysical first principles. The laws of nature are known as laws because they satisfy the requirements of method, not because they can be traced to or lead to some metaphysical principle. In short, methodology and metaphysics are mutually exclusive.

Let's support this conclusion by considerations following a different route. Descartes speaks of laws of nature as governing matter, but what is matter? That issue belongs to physics, which he says is too controversial to discuss in the *Discourse*. That's his familiar striptease again: the most fundamental things are the things he can't talk about. He does, however, tell us crucial aspects of his doctrine, namely, in Part 4: when he speaks of the object of the geometers, he speaks of it not only as extended in length, breadth, and depth, but also as moving. The object of the geometers, in short, is simply the extension of the world, or "all my physics is part of geometry," as he says elsewhere. But what of this extension? Is it simple or compound? After all, any extension that we encounter is a compound body, capable of division; it normally does, in fact it always does divide. What are its parts? Are these ultimate parts atoms, or is extension infinitely divisible? What are the ultimate parts, if any? Descartes's position is quite evident here from the silence: we can know the laws of nature without answering the question of the nature of the ultimate parts. The metaphysical ultimacy is unnecessary. That separates in its essential character this apparently very materialist physical doctrine from the materialist physics of, say, a Lucretius, which absolutely derives from the discovery of the ultimate particles. This is the modern concept of nature. Descartes does not know the ultimate parts. Newton insisted, "I don't know the ultimate parts; I don't need to for the sake of my three fundamental laws of motion." No one today knows the ultimate parts either. Of course, the more we discover about the parts or particles, the more we have to revise the laws. Nature lacks finality. And if we don't know the ultimate parts, we certainly do not have a concept of the whole, of nature as a whole.

If man ceases to have a relationship to the whole, then what becomes crucial to him is his relationship to other men. This is the premise, you can say, of the politicization of philosophy. We have caught a glimpse of it in Part 6: philosophy or science joining together with the body politic in the mastery of nature for the alleviation of the human condition.

We can now put the right questions to our starting point, Descartes's statement of his goal, mastery of nature. This goal sounds amazingly contemporary in the twentieth century, provided, of course, we substitute "science" for "philosophy." It is already clear in Part 6 that Descartes proposes what has become a realized fact for us. Science has become a function of society, of its needs and goals, for instance. Conversely, society is constantly dependent on science, for its well being, for its standard of living, for its military defense, and so on. Now it is not my purpose here to draw up one more balance sheet of goods and evils of this project of modern science. As students of philosophy we should note at least that the quest for understanding has lost its former directedness toward transcending the political, and standing in a relationship to the whole and to that which is always. As regards political society, it has lost its fundamental characteristic as a self-sufficient community in charge of its own well-being. Its technological goals and its military security depend on a world community of scientists.

But as students of the *Discourse*, we have to ask this final question. Has this bond between philosophy or science and society been shown to be reasonable? If we cast our eye over the whole of the *Discourse on Method*, we can see that everything in Descartes's thought depends on his weaving together two quite distinct strands. Initially, he sought certainty for the sake of utility. The utility theme, the good or end for man, is throughout governed by the natural egoism, the premise that man naturally seeks his own good, which means, with all due refinement, his own pleasure. Descartes does, of course, state what sounds like a categorical law of obligation in the early part of Part 6. There is a law, he says, that obliges us to benefit other men to the degree to which it is in our power. If we note carefully, however, all the instances of the word "oblige" in Part 6, we see that he revises this categorical obligation and makes it a hypothetical obligation: If you are virtuous, that is, if you desire to benefit other men in ways possible through your science, then you are obliged. To do what? Well, to support science, experiment, exchange experiments, and so on. In short, the categorical character of the obligation simply recedes into the hedonistic or utilitarian goal. That concludes the utility theme. The other theme, the certainty theme, is spelled out in terms of mathematics, that is to say, mathematical method and mathematical physics. The utility theme and the certainty theme as articulated are irreducible to each other. That's really the key, I think, to understanding this methodology. We recognize that irreducibility in a certain way today. It is the same heterogeneity of human experience and scientific laws that is the great theme of certain twentieth-century philosophers, for example, Whitehead in *Science and the Modern World*. The irreducibility of these two strands to each other means that they are in principle disparate. Descartes does not really say that the determination of the answer to the question "what is the right life for man?" must be based upon scientific knowledge. His reflection here is entirely in terms of human experience. We can separate these heterogeneous strands, and that is the liberating fact that we learn from the *Discourse*. We are free to interpret the nature of science in ways other than mastery of nature. We are free to learn from science while recognizing its limitations. Here, in Descartes, science does not know the ultimate, the particles; it does not know the whole. As scientific knowledge, it does not comprehend the human. If reinterpreted within these limits, its knowledge may well be an immense benefaction. But since it knows neither the whole nor the human part, we are free to philosophize independently of Cartesian and modern science.

GLOSSARY

Algebra (*algèbre*). See **Logic, Geometrical Analysis, Algebra**.

Appetite (*appétit*) is a classification for certain feelings or sensations (*sentiments*) such as hunger and thirst that impel us to seek what will benefit us and avoid what is harmful. It is distinguished from **Reason** and thus from **Clear and Distinct (Ideas)**. In the last paragraph of the *Treatise on Man* (1629-33; summarized in Part 5 of the *Discourse on Method*), appetites are attributed to the body-machine alone, but appetite also belongs to a **True Man**, Descartes tells us in the last paragraph of Part 5 of the *Discourse*. (See also **Passion**)

Architecture (*architecture*) is an image or model for the well-founded methodical approach; but the word "fruits" is also used to describe the results of the approach.

Art (*art*) is sometimes used pejoratively, as in Part 2, where native gifts are superior to instruction; but it is also an image of the project of Cartesian philosophy.

Beasts (*bêtes*). Descartes reserves this term for nonhuman animals, which do not possess soul but are only bodies or body-machines.

Body (*corps*). Descartes uses this word to denote (1) the human body in general or one's own body in particular, as, for example, in Part 5 when he describes the circulation of the blood; (2) the "object of the geometers," which he describes towards the end of Part 4 as "a continuous body, or a space indefinitely extended," a meaning he often identifies with **Matter**, as in chapter 6 of *The World* (1629-33); (3) any corporeal object. (See also **Matter**)

Certain, Certainty (*certain, certitude*). Certainty is a condition of mind in which one is sure of what one thinks or believes. For Descartes, certainty belongs to what is impervious to doubt. In its most rigorous sense, it means what cannot be rationally doubted or doubted without contradiction. Descartes also recognizes a less rigorous sense, which he calls moral certainty or moral assurance, the kind of certainty we usually have for our actions in daily life, as in Part 4, paragraph 7. (See also **Clear and Distinct**)

Clear and Distinct (Ideas) (*clair* or *nette, distinct*). Descartes's arrival at something indubitable in Part 4 leads him to identify characteristics of what is certain—it is clear and distinct. He does not explain these terms in the *Discourse on Method,* and gives only a brief account in *Principles of Philosophy* (1644), section 45. By "clear" he means vividly present to mind; by "distinct" he means separated off from anything that does not belong to it or render it lucid. He often uses the adverb rather than adjective; what is more, he acknowledges degrees of clarity and of distinctness. The term "clear and distinct evidence" became a catchphrase for the Cartesian requirement of scientific knowledge. (See also **Certain, Certainty**)

Content, Contentment (*content, contentement*). Contentment is a feeling that reflects the general character of one's life, one's ability to remain calm and secure amid life's disturbances. (See also **Satisfaction**)

Deduce (*déduire*). Descartes uses this term in both a strong and a weak sense. In the strong sense, it means (as a verb) an inferring from something that is known with certainty to something else that necessarily follows from it, or (as a noun, "deduction") that which we know as a result of a necessary inference. There is a strong statement of this in Rule 3 of *Rules for the Direction of the Native Intelligence* (1628). Descartes also uses it in a weak sense, in the case of inferences in which the requirement of necessity does not appear to be as stringent, for example, in Part 5, where he acknowledges that particular effects can be deduced from general principles in "several different ways" and may require evidence from experiment.

Disposition (*disposition*). We have translated this word most often as "arrangement," since Descartes usually means by it a particular organization or structure of the body (the human body most often), as in bodily organs. The term is used very frequently in the *Treatise on Man* (1629-33) and in Part 5.

Doubt (*doute*). In Part 1, Descartes uses this word in its most ordinary meaning, as uncertainty of mind, for example, when he confesses to having "many doubts" about what he had learned; however, because he employs doubt as a means of inquiry, we can distinguish two other, related senses of the word. In Part 2 he chooses to adjust all his opinions to the "standard of reason" and places that standard (clarity and distinctness) as the first rule of his methodical procedure; and in Part 4 he undertakes exactly this adjustment by means of doubt. This we can call methodical doubt. Late in Part 4, however, he states that the truth of what is clear and distinct depends on the existence and perfection of God, implying, perhaps, a doubt of the methodical principle itself, sometimes called metaphysical doubt. The possibility of that doubt is explored not here but in *Meditations on First Philosophy* (1641).

Evidence, Evident, Evidently (*évidence, évident, évidemment*). To count as evidence, something must be obvious or conspicuous. Descartes most often restricts the term to matters that are obvious when present to the **Mind**; that is to say, matters that show themselves as obvious, and even undeniable, when simply thought about.

Experience, Experiment (*expérience*). The French word may mean either experience or experiment. Although experiment does not make an appearance in the methodical rules of Part 2, Descartes tells us at the end of Part 2 that he accumulated experiments so as to think them over. Experiments are controlled inquiries in which particular phenomena are tested and examined. The notion of experiment has a prominent role in Parts 5 and 6, where it is a requirement for his continued progress in knowledge.

Faith (*foi*). Descartes counts "truths of faith" or religion among his beliefs and exempts them from doubt. They appear to be outside the scope of reason.

Fortune (*fortune*). Whether chance, luck, or circumstances that befall us, in the *Discourse* fortune is contrasted with "the will of men using reason" in Part 2, and is the specific subject of the third moral maxim in Part 3. (See also **Method**)

Foundation (*fondement*). Descartes exposes his previous opinions, even those that seem to be obvious, as doubtful. The insecure bases of these dubitable opinions (our senses, habits, and customs, for example) must be replaced with a firm and secure basis or foundation for knowledge or philosophy, that is to say, indubitable truth. (See also **Method**)

Geometrical Analysis (*l'analyse des géomètres*). See **Logic, Geometrical Analysis, Algebra**.

God (*Dieu*). Descartes acknowledges the varieties of religions and of gods, but focuses primarily on the God of Christian theology, who is seen as a perfect being and a foundation of Cartesian metaphysics. God's perfections include infinity, eternity, omniscience, and immutability (see Part 4). Descartes attempts a proof of God's existence in Part 4, and in Part 5 he proposes a different version of creation than that which appears in the Bible. God can be understood as having established laws of nature to which the matter that God created is obedient.

Human (*humain*). The human being, composed of two principles—soul or mind and body—is distinguished both from the **Beasts**, which are only bodies or machines, and from **God**, the divine or perfect Being, who is neither bodily nor composite. The presence of soul or reason distinguishes us as human. (But see also **Beasts, Soul, True Man**)

Imagination (*imagination*). In the *Discourse*, the imagination is the ability to have images and, along with sensation, is the source of dubitable opinions or thoughts. In earlier and later writings (the *Rules for the Direction of the Native Intelligence* [1628] and *Meditations on First Philosophy* [1641]) its connection to the body is stressed and it is given a role in fashioning, for example, mathematical symbols.

Laws (*lois*). In Part 2 where Descartes is reflecting on kinds of perfection before thinking about how to proceed in his own philosophy, he calls upon law as it governs human doing, as in political legislation and laws of religion. In Part 5 he proposes that all matter moves according to laws of nature and identifies the laws of nature with the rules of mechanics. In Part 6 he invokes a law that obliges us to seek the good of mankind. (See also **Rule**)

Logic, Geometrical Analysis, Algebra (*logique, l'analyse des géomètres, algebra*). **Logic** here is the syllogistic logic developed from Aristotle's logical writings, called the *Organon*, by medieval logicians. The syllogism is a form of reasoning consisting of three propositions (called respectively the major premise, the minor premise, and the conclusion). An example commonly used is the following: All men are mortal (major premise); Socrates is a man (minor premise); therefore, Socrates is mortal (conclusion). If the premises are true, the conclusion must be true. Descartes, like Francis Bacon before him (see *New Organon* [1620] 1.11-14), charges that the syllogism does not allow us to discover anything new. **Geometrical Analysis** refers to a procedure for solving geometrical problems in use by the ancients. Pappus (fl. A.D. 320) writes that it is "a special body of doctrine provided for the use of those who, after finishing the ordinary Elements, are desirous of acquiring the power of solving problems which may be set them involving [the construction of] lines." See T. L. Heath's edition of Euclid's *Elements*, volume 1 (New York: Dover, 1956), 138. Pappus identifies Euclid, Apollonius of Perga, and Aristaeus the elder as the authors of this art. See Heath's remarks about its obscurity in volume 3 (246). François Viète (1540-1603) thought he found traces of an impure **Algebra** in Euclid, Apollonius, Pappus, and Diophantus. An example of the kind of algebra with which Descartes was acquainted can be found in Viète's *Introduction to the Analytic Art*, translated as an appendix in Jacob Klein, *Greek Mathematical Thought and the Origin of Algebra*, translated by Eva Brann (Cambridge: MIT Press, 1968).

Master (*maître*). Descartes uses the word in its then-contemporary sense of teacher or artisan in Part 1, and the reflection on **Perfection** that begins Part 2 singles out masters. In Part 6, he promises that his philosophy will make us "like masters and possessors of nature." (See also **Fortune**)

Metaphysics (*métaphysique*). Descartes uses this term in three distinct ways: (1) in its adjectival form it sometimes means very lofty and difficult (see, for example, Part 4, paragraph 1); (2) it refers to the metaphysics or science of being of the tradition coming mainly from Aristotle but also from Platonic sources through the **Schools**; (3) he calls his own account of the soul and God in Part 4 metaphysics. In the later *Meditations on First Philosophy* (1641) he addresses metaphysical topics more amply.

Method (*méthode*). Descartes's claim is that he cannot trust most of what he once accepted as true or certain, which indicates that his thinking has been errant. He designs method to overcome this errancy by correcting or removing any tendency or habit of relying on mere opinion or dubitable thinking either as a foundation or as a procedure of reasoning. Method is a means or procedure for thinking that has a secure **Foundation**. It allows one to conduct one's reason well and seek for truth. In Part 1, Descartes says it is a means to augment knowledge and elevate it to the highest degree possible. In Part 2, he formulates four **Rules** that he sometimes refers to as method. (See also **Usefulness**)

Mind (*esprit*). This term is frequently used in its most general sense as interchangeable with **Soul**, and thus is distinguished from **Body**. It refers to the cognitive power understood to be consciousness or awareness, and to the rational power to lay hold of indubitable truths. Descartes recognizes two classes of soul or mind: strong minds (*esprits forts*), who are capable of resiliency and resoluteness; and weak minds (*esprits faibles*), who are less so (see Part 3, paragraphs 2 and 3, and Part 5, final paragraph). By contrast, Descartes also uses the word *esprit* in a physiological sense (see Part 5), to refer to very quickly moving rarified bodies, which he calls animal spirits. In this he is following contemporary physiological terminology. Thus Descartes's animal spirits are not souls.

Morality (*morale*). The word in French can mean moral doctrine or ethics. In the brief introductory summary to the *Discourse*, Descartes claims that his moral rules are drawn from the **Method**, yet the moral doctrine he offers is a "provisional" one consisting of four maxims.

Natural Light (*lumière naturelle*). Although the term "natural light" occurs only once in the *Discourse*, it is mentioned often in the later *Meditations on First Philosophy* (1641). It refers to **Reason** understood as inborn or native capacity to discern the truth, and thus is a natural basis for escaping the deceptions to which we are susceptible, once it is supplemented with **Method**.

Nature (*nature*). We can discern two senses of nature at work in the *Discourse*. The first adopts the term from traditional **Metaphysics**, where it means essence or form. Thus Descartes argues in Part 4 that **Soul** is a substance whose nature is to think. The second identifies nature with **Matter** and all things constituted by matter and motion, and in this use of the word, nature is distinct from soul.

Opinion (*opinion*). A general term for any uncritically accepted belief.

Order (*ordre*). To proceed by means of **Method** requires that one conduct inquiries in an orderly way, that is to say, following certain rules and a certain sequence. As Descartes describes it in the third rule of Part 2, the order of inquiry moves from what is simplest and easiest to know and proceeds step by step to what is more difficult or more complex. At the opening of Part 2, he tells us that a project designed by one person is more ordered than that in which many have a hand. In Part 5, God is said to have created **Matter** and its motion without order.

Passion (*passion*). Passions are excitations of the soul, including not only love, hate, anger, and so on, but also courage, emulation, remorse, and other feelings. In Descartes's last writing, *The Passions of the Soul* (1649), he says they are "caused, maintained, and strengthened" by movement of the animal spirits (Article 27) and "incite and dispose their soul to will the things for which they prepare their body" (Article 40). In Part 5 of the *Discourse*, hunger and thirst are treated as "internal passions."

Perfect, Perfection (*parfait, perfection*). Descartes begins Part 2 by reflecting on perfection, considering buildings, towns, and laws both political and religious. Here perfection involves primarily being well ordered to a single purpose by a single person. In Part 4, after establishing the first principle of his philosophy, he reflects again on perfection, this time about the imperfection of his own being in relation to that of **God**, who possesses infinite perfections, such as eternity, omniscience, and omnipotence. Descartes there makes the idea of perfection the basis of an argument for God's existence.

Philosophy (*philosophie*). Most often Descartes uses this term to refer to the dubitable philosophy handed down in the learned tradition, but he also uses it of his own philosophy, which is meant to replace it.

Physics (*physique*). Physics is the science of nature understood by Descartes as the science of matter in motion. Matter moves according to the laws of nature and can be described by mathematics. His science of physics is meant to replace the science of nature or physics built on Aristotelian principles.

Public (*public*). Descartes sees previous philosophy as the activity of a small group of learned persons only. By contrast his philosophy is important to the public and is addressed to the public, as we see from the fact that it is written in French rather than Latin, the language of the **Schools**.

Reason (*raison*). "Reason" often means the power to know clear and distinct truths apart from any reliance on the senses or imagination. It is this meaning that is usually associated with the argument of Part 4, and with the project to adjust all things to the level of reason; however, "reason" also means a power wider in function, the universal instrument that is useful in all sorts of circumstances, discussed in paragraph 10 of Part 5.

Reformation (*réformation*). Part of Descartes's purpose is reformation of the sciences or disciplines of learning. In Part 2 he qualifies the extent of the reform he is undertaking, by claiming it is not political, as well as the persons who should undertake such a thing; in Part 3, the reform may extend to **Morality**.

Resolution (*résolution*). This word and its verbal forms are linked to strong minds and to firmness of will. (See also **Mind**)

Rule (*règle*). The prescriptions of **Method** are called rules, since they are meant as principles to be applied in the conduct of reason. Descartes had attempted to spell out his philosophy as a set of rules in the early *Rules for the Direction of the Native Intelligence* (1628). The **Morality** of Part 3 also has rules.

Satisfaction (*satisfaction*). This term is used primarily for the pleasure that attends a particular circumstance or outcome. (See also **Contentment**)

Schools (*écoles*). This term refers to the institutional repository of the tradition, the academies or centers of learning. The terms mentioned in Part 1, paragraph 2, are taken over from Aristotelian philosophy. *Accidents* or accidental properties are those that may or may not belong to a being. They are distinguished from essential properties, properties that must belong to the being. By *form*, according to Étienne Gilson (*Discours de la méthode, texte et commentaire*, sixth edition [Paris: Vrin, 1987], 89), is meant substantial form: beings of our experience are regarded as unities composed of form (*eidos*) and material (*hyle*). Substantial form is the active principle that when united to material constitutes with it a natural body, that is to say, a being that has within it a principle of motion and rest. One meaning of *nature* in the tradition is this principle of motion and rest within the being, and each such being is said to have a nature. *Individual* refers to the singular being as distinct from the species to which it belongs; and *species* is what can be said of many beings insofar as they differ only numerically.

Science (*science*). Descartes uses this word to refer sometimes to the established disciplines of learning, sometimes to the body of knowledge he hopes to establish. Descartes seeks science that is both certain and useful, as he tells us in Part 1. **Method** is a means to science, yet in Descartes's own science we can distinguish a rigorous sense, where certainty is primary and the claim is sometimes that we can have rigorous deduction, from a sense that includes the necessity for **Experiment** and even for models or analogies.

Soul (*âme*). This term is used interchangeably with **Mind**. Descartes distinguishes soul from what is nonsouled or bodily; that is to say, he distinguishes the rational power from the natural or corporeally constituted things, like **Beasts** and **Machines**. Descartes's account constitutes a revision in the meaning of soul that had been handed down. (In general, soul had been understood as the principle of life, motion, and awareness.) The discovery of the circulation of the blood played an important part in that revision. He also distinguishes among souls in terms of strength and weakness. (See also **Mind**)

Substance (*substance*). This is a term from the Aristotelian metaphysical tradition, commonly used in the **Schools**, which Descartes employs in Part 4 to characterize the soul. He defines the term in the *Second Replies* to the *Meditations on First Philosophy* (1641). It applies "to every thing in which whatever we perceive immediately resides, as in a subject, or to every thing by means of which whatever we perceive exists."

Theology (*théologie*). The study or science of the divine being.

True Man (*vrai homme*). After having argued that soul and body are entirely distinct from one another in Part 4, Descartes uses the term "true man" twice in Part 5 (paragraphs 10 and 12), both times indicating that a true man is a union between soul and body.

Use, Usefulness (*utilité*). In the *Discourse* Descartes stresses that the philosophy he proposes has a different aim than the "speculative philosophy...taught in the schools." His philosophy is "practical," that is to say, "useful for life" or beneficial, and will make us "like masters and possessors of nature."

Virtue, Vice (*vertu, vice*). Descartes gives no definition of virtue or vice in the *Discourse*. He mentions virtue in his critique of his education in Part 1 and in Part 3 tells us that if we judge as best we can, we can "acquire all the virtues together with all the other goods that one can acquire" and thus "cannot fail to be content."

INDEX